PERSPECTIVES ON AID AND DEVELOPMENT

T0306941

POLICY ESSAY NO. 22

PERSPECTIVES ON AID AND DEVELOPMENT

Edited by Catherine Gwin and Joan M. Nelson

Elliot Berg
Michael Bruno
Paul Collier
Martin Ravallion
Lyn Squire

Distributed by the Johns Hopkins University Press
Published by the Overseas Development Council
Washington, DC

Copyright © 1997 by Overseas Development Council, Washington, DC

Distributed by:
The Johns Hopkins University Press
2715 North Charles Street
Baltimore, MD 21218-4319

All rights reserved under International and Pan-American Conventions. No part of this book may be reproduced or transmitted in any form or by any means, electronic or mechanical, including photocopying, recording, or any information storage and retrieval system, without prior permission in writing from the publisher. All inquiries should be addressed to the Copyright Clearance Center, 222 Rosewood Drive, Danvers, MA 01923.

Library of Congress Cataloging-In-Publication Data

Gwin, Catherine and Joan M. Nelson
Perspectives on Aid and Development/Catherine Gwin and Joan M. Nelson

Policy Essay No. 22
Includes bibliographic references.

p. cm. (Policy Essay: No. 22)
Includes bibliographic references.
1. Economic assistance—Developing countries. 2. Developing countries—Economic policy. I. Gwin, Catherine. II. Series.

HC60.P3927 1997 338.91′09172—dc21 97-29209 CIP

ISBN: 1-56517-007-5

Printed in the United States of America.

Editor: Jacqueline Edlund-Braun
Cover design: Ripe Studios

The views expressed in this volume are those of the authors and do not necessarily represent those of the Overseas Development Council as an organization or of its individual officers, Board, Council, advisory groups, and staff members.

Contents

Foreword

It is often said today that development aid is in crisis. A more constructive, and more accurate, view is that development aid is in a period of major transition. No longer is aid the predominant source of development financing or the predominant mode of interaction between economies of the North and South, nor should it be for most developing countries. But neither has the time for development aid passed.

Far more than at any previous point in the last several decades, both donor and developing countries are in more general accord about the broad approaches required to foster sustained, poverty-reducing growth and development. Yet, paradoxically, there is now much uncertainty and skepticism among donors and recipients alike about the role and influence of development aid in helping countries move in desired directions. In part for this reason, faith in, and support for, official development assistance is diminishing at the very time that its potential for significant positive impact should be at an all time high.

In *Perspectives on Aid and Development,* distinguished policy experts offer perspectives on the lessons learned from development experience and how these lessons have been translated into new thinking on aid and development issues.

In the introduction, ODC Senior Vice President Catherine Gwin and Senior Associate Joan M. Nelson synthesize the several strands of "new thinking" presented by the following chapters and set the stage for the discussion of the two potentials in development aid—for a broad and deep consensus on development strategies, and for increased aid effectiveness in supporting countries' development efforts.

Michael Bruno, Martin Ravallion, and Lyn Squire, all of the World Bank, use recent major improvements in the measurement of trends in household income to re-examine the relation between growth and equity. They conclude that there is little evidence that growth increases inequality, but compelling evidence that growth reduces poverty—and does so more effectively if pro-growth policies are accompanied by pro-poor measures.

However, Paul Collier, Professor of Economics and Director of Oxford University's Centre for the Study of African Economies, challenges the widely held assumption that aid and conditionality can influence policies. Aid can effectively support growth and poverty reduction, he insists, only in certain contexts: selectivity, not conditionality, is the key.

Development economist Elliot Berg closely examines five contradictions in the aid process itself that dilute its effectiveness in both the medium term (by impeding local commitment and ownership) and the long term (by undermining institutional development and capacity building). Aid strategies need radical revision, including orderly reductions in those countries which are extremely aid-dependent.

Perspectives on Aid and Development follows in a long tradition of ODC publications concerned with the development aid challenge. Most recently, ODC published *Improving Aid to Africa* by Nicolas van de Walle, which presented the policy findings of a collaborative project of field research and analyses of donor/African relations and how African countries use aid resources. Earlier in the Policy Essay series, ODC explored the scope and limitations of conditionality in several volumes: *Global Goals, Contentious Means: Issues of Multiple Aid Conditionality*, by Joan Nelson with Stephanie Eglinton; *Pro-Poor Aid Conditionality*, by John P. Lewis; *Pressing for Peace: Can Aid Induce Reform?* by Nicole Ball; and *Encouraging Democracy: The Politics of Economic Adjustment*, by Joan Nelson with Stephanie Eglinton.

Perspectives on Aid and Development was made possible by the generous support of The Ford Foundation and The Rockefeller Foundation. ODC gratefully acknowledges their support for its overall program.

John W. Sewell
President
October 1997

Perspectives on Aid and Development

POLICY ESSAY NO. 22

Introduction

Development and Aid: New Evidence and New Issues

Catherine Gwin and Joan M. Nelson

The basis exists today for a broader consensus on development strategies than at any time in many decades. Almost 20 years of experience with economic policy reforms plus expanded data and analysis on that experience provide the foundation for a strengthened accord both within and among developing and developed countries. Beyond the wide recognition that prevails on the need for countries to get their macroeconomic fundamentals right, there are now grounds for agreement on an even wider range of issues entailed in achieving sustainable, poverty-reducing growth and social development. This does not mean that all policy debates have been resolved. They never will be, since beyond certain fundamentals many of the answers to how countries can best grow and develop will reflect variations in underlying conditions and values. Nonetheless, the experience and knowledge gained ought to bring to a close some of the most contentious debates of past years on growth and poverty reduction.

In an era of rapidly expanding information, trade, and capital flows, an expanded consensus on development strategies should usher in a "grand era" of development cooperation. Yet new assessments of development assistance efforts make clear that important issues have to be addressed by donor and recipient countries if aid's potential for effectively supporting the new consensus is to be realized.

This introduction and the three essays that follow address these two potentials—for a broad and deep consensus on development strategies, and for increased aid effectiveness in supporting countries' development efforts. The essays, each of which are drawn from presentations first made elsewhere, are reprinted here because they present major strands of the current analysis on development strategies and aid. While their diagnoses have certain points in common, their recommendations differ in significant ways. Taken together, they pose a number of key questions for the future of development aid policy.

The first essay, by Michael Bruno, Martin Ravallion, and Lyn Squire, focuses on development strategies more than on development aid, although it draws implications from its analysis about how aid resources should be used. Importantly, it pulls together evidence regarding one of the most contentious issues of the development debate in the 1980s—specifically, the impact of growth and growth-promoting economic reforms on poverty and inequality in developing countries. It also offers new and important insights into how initial conditions of inequality in countries may affect both growth and the speed with which growth can foster a reduction in poverty.

The other two essays, by Paul Collier and Elliot Berg, focus on the role of aid. Their arguments are consistent with the general development analysis laid out by Bruno and his colleagues. However, their two different sets of recommendations for improving the impact of aid raise challenging questions about how development aid can best be programmed to support efforts consistent with this analysis.

This overview presents 1) a brief description of the changed development policy context from which the Bruno et al. essay emerges as a capstone of years of debate; 2) a short review of the evolution of the aid effectiveness issue, including a comparison of Collier's and Berg's approaches to improving the impact of aid; and 3) identification of key questions that face the development community in arriving at an effective aid strategy that builds on lessons learned about development and aid policies.

THE EVOLVING CONSENSUS ON GROWTH AND POVERTY REDUCTION STRATEGIES

■ DOMINANT THEORIES of development have evolved through several phases since economic development of poorer countries became an international concern in the first decades after World War II. Two main themes can be distinguished: ideas regarding what makes economies grow, and prevailing views regarding how to best reduce poverty. Changing ideas on both topics and their interrelationships in turn shaped approaches to aid.

In the 1950s and 1960s, economic theories emphasized the accumulation of capital as the driving engine of growth. Growth, in turn, was viewed as the key to poverty reduction. A large public sector was seen as the essential counter to weak markets and private sector forces.

By the end of the 1960s, however, confidence in the trickle-down approach to poverty reduction had waned because progress was so slow. In the early 1970s, the United States and other bilateral donors turned to more proactive approaches to combatting poverty, emphasizing directly addressing basic human needs.[1] By mid-decade, the World Bank, until then largely focused on infrastructure, began to devote much more analysis and lending to direct efforts to reduce poverty, and several bilateral donors began pursuing distinct pro-poor development efforts.

At the same time, however, a deep rift began to appear regarding how to promote and sustain growth. The earlier consensus was challenged by the two oil price shocks, sharply increased commercial borrowing and debt, growing evidence of the exhaustion of the prevailing import substitution growth strategy in Latin America, and slowed growth or stagnation in much of Africa. In many developing countries, the conviction grew that the fundamental obstacles to growth were the biased national and international laws and institutions of the rich world and the rapacious behavior of multinational corporations and international banks. Those convictions prompted increasingly strident calls for a New International Economic Order. Meanwhile, some analysts and development specialists in Europe and the United States were becoming increasingly critical of the policies and practices of many developing country governments. That perspective was perhaps most clearly signaled by the 1981 World Bank report, *Accelerated Development in Sub-Saharan Africa.* The "Berg Report," as it is commonly called, argued strongly that stagnation and decline already evident in much of Africa reflected the domestic economic policies and behavior of governments, rather than adverse international price trends or other external forces.[2]

Thus, by the early 1980s, even before the international debt crisis broke, major donor agencies began to offer non-project aid conditioned on macroeconomic policy reforms. Mexico's default on its external debts in August 1982 and the debt crisis that followed focused attention still more sharply on macroeconomic stabilization measures and liberalization, especially of financial markets and external trade.

The design of policy reforms emphasized market-based policy fundamentals: fiscal discipline is a crucial precondition for growth; growth is best advanced through markets rather than state intervention and through open economies and export promotion rather than import substitution and industrial policies. This approach reflected many influences, including the dramatic growth of the East Asian "tigers," contrasted with chronic inflationary pressures and populist cycles in Latin America and with stagnation in Sub-Saharan Africa. Despite quite different origins, the new conventional wisdom coincided with the rising tide of opposition to "big government" in the United States and the United Kingdom.

The new paradigm initially provoked bitter controversy and resistance. In most developing countries, it challenged long-established ideological leanings and perceptions and threatened deeply entrenched systems of political patronage and powerful vested economic interests. Yet, in the course of the 1980s and the early 1990s, its core elements gradually prevailed. Acceptance was widened by failed heterodox attempts to stabilize and resume growth (as in Brazil and Peru in the mid-1980s), by the increasingly impressive economic performance of Chile, and most dramatically by the collapse of Communism in the Soviet Union and Eastern Europe in 1989–1990. By the early 1990s, the crucial importance of fiscal discipline; the advantages of market-determined prices, interest rates, and exchange rates; and the benefits of trade liberalization—all issues on which there was profound disagreement in the early 1980s—were increasingly accepted in much of the world. So too, in broad principle, were the merits of a limited public sector role in direct economic activities—though differences have remained on the particulars of such issues as financial and regulatory reforms, industrial policy, and the extent of privatization.

Growing acceptance of the paradigm also reflected some revision of its more extreme positions in the late 1980s and 1990s. In the mid-1980s, some (mainly Washington-centered) rhetoric seemed to endorse the philosophy "that government is best which governs least." Just two or three years later, the World Bank was beginning to emphasize the crucial role of good governance as an element in promoting growth—not only because markets do not perform all functions well, but because well-functioning public laws, regulations, and institutions are essential for well-functioning markets.[3] Deepened understanding in the 1990s of the East Asian experience strongly reinforced this point. By the mid-1990s, "reform of the state"—increased efficiency and responsiveness, reduced corruption, and a narrower but vigorous array of functions—was high on the political agenda of many countries in Latin America and much of Africa, South Asia, and the post-Communist world.

By the late 1980s, a different position regarding poverty reduction was also emerging. In the first few years of the debt crisis, overriding preoccupation with restoring international financial stability essentially sidelined poverty concerns in many but not all countries and in their interactions with the international financial institutions (though not all bilateral aid agencies). As it became clear that stabilization and structural adjustment would take years, and as the social costs of protracted economic crisis became painfully evident, nongovernmental organizations (NGOs) within and outside reforming countries together with UNICEF led growing demands that adjustment programs include safety nets and compensatory programs to buffer the most vulnerable groups.[4] In response, discussions within countries and discussions between the international financial institutions (notably the World Bank and the International Monetary Fund) and their client countries began to address how education, health, and other social sectors should be sheltered from austerity-induced budget cuts. However, this return to poverty concerns remained limited primarily to measures to deal with the short-term costs of adjustment. It was not until the 1990s, that the convergence of a wider set of factors brought a comprehensive concern with poverty reduction back to the center stage of development efforts.

In 1990, the publication of the World Bank's *World Development Report* on poverty signaled this restoration of poverty reduction to its 1970s status as the central long-run goal of development and aid.[5] By then it was abundantly clear that despite modest or in a few cases robust revival of economic growth in countries which were engaging in economic reforms, poverty remained pervasive and deep. Indeed, poverty had become both more widespread and more acute in much of Africa and Latin America during the 1980s. Resumed and accelerated growth was imperative to reduce poverty. But beyond growth, explicit pro-poor policies and programs were also needed. The key measures, the World Bank argued, were policies and institutions designed to promote productive use of the poor's most abundant asset—labor—through increased employment and access to credit, and a vigorous effort to assure that the poor have access to basic social services, above all health and education. In the next several years, the World Bank, the Inter-American Development Bank, and the Asian Development Bank rapidly increased the share of their resources focused on human resource development and social sector programs.

Despite the sharply increased attention and resources targeted on reducing poverty, and despite resumed growth in many developing and post-Communist countries, unemployment, poverty, inequality, and crumbling social services remain widespread. Many believe these problems are caused, or at least exacerbated by stabilization, structural adjustment, and neo-liberal growth strategies. Seven years after the World Bank's major report on poverty, intense debate continues as to whether poverty is indeed dwindling, and if not, why.

The debate is fed by the tension between two sets of data. One set shows that the absolute number of poor people in the world (and in all developing regions except East Asia) continues to increase as population grows. (Even today a quarter of the world's population still lives in conditions of severe poverty and deprivation; some 1.3 billion of these poor people eke out a life on incomes of less than a $1 a day.) The second set of facts demonstrates that the proportion of poor people has nonetheless shrunk dramatically. It also documents improvements in other indicators of well-being, such as access to basic education and health care, infant and child mortality, and life expectancy.

These competing (though not contradictory) facts have prompted persistent questions and doubts. To what degree can we expect growth to reduce poverty in the absence of specific pro-poor policies and programs? Do stabilization and adjustment measures increase poverty in the short and medium run, even if they also promote growth and reduce poverty in the long run? Do stabilization and growth increase inequality, not only by their effects on the poor but also by further enriching the wealthy?

Recent data and analysis provide much clearer answers to these questions than were available earlier.[6] The discussion by Michael Bruno and his colleagues in this volume distills many recent findings.

The first set of findings relates to the effect of growth on inequality. Specifically, comparable and comprehensive measurements of income distribution in 45 countries from the 1960s to the 1990s demonstrate that there is no systematic impact—one way or the other—of growth on inequality. In general, growth is found to be "distribution-neutral," benefiting all layers of society roughly in proportion to their initial levels of living. Sustained rapid growth virtually always reduces poverty; indeed, even modest overall growth can often generate quite significant reductions in the proportion of people in absolute poverty, particularly where much of the population is clustered close to the poverty line. Pro-poor policies and programs enhance the effectiveness of growth in reducing poverty. But the best data give little support to the pessimistic belief that when countries grow, poverty is undiminished.

Second, the evidence shows that stabilization and adjustment measures have more mixed impacts on the poor than either the proponents or the critics of adjustment have argued. Moreover, it is extremely difficult to untangle the effects of economic crisis and depression—that is, the reasons why adjustment measures are undertaken—from the early impact of the adjustment measures themselves. As would be expected, recession increased poverty virtually everywhere. Inequality also increased sharply in Eastern Europe. In Latin America, in contrast, the evidence is more mixed.[7] In Africa, stagnant or shrinking production greatly increased poverty, but specific stabilization and structural changes had mixed short-term effects. Some of the poor may even have been helped directly and immediately (for example, even before growth was rekindled). Indeed, the most extensive and careful analysis to date found that trade and exchange rate reforms led to declines in economic rents and shifts in relative prices that favored the rural and urban poor.[8]

More specifically, different components of adjustment have been shown to have different effects on the poor. High or hyper-inflation is particularly hard on the poor, who are least able to shield themselves from skyrocketing prices. Successful price stabilization therefore benefits almost everyone, and, contrary to widely held views, especially the poor. Other elements of adjustment have more mixed effects, depending on the sectors of the economy in which the poor are concentrated, the expenditures the government chooses to cut most severely, and other factors. Deregulation and liberalization directly hurt some among the poor and directly help others (for instance, they help small-scale producers of export crops whose earnings have been squeezed by commodity board monopolies). Not surprisingly, the poor fare better overall where the economy rebounds rapidly after deep crisis.

In short, Bruno and his co-authors' second basic message is this: growth is necessary to sustained poverty reduction; structural adjustment is necessary (though, especially in the poorest countries, not sufficient) for growth; and the costs of adjustment can be substantially mitigated and the benefits of growth enhanced by pro-poor policies.

The chapter also reviews a third set of findings, focused not on how growth and adjustment affect poverty and inequality, but on how inequality affects growth and poverty reduction. Growth, they find, reduces poverty more rapidly in countries with comparatively equal income distributions than in countries with high inequality. In addition, new evidence suggests that countries with very unequal distributions of income or assets (especially land) may grow more slowly, though the data remain to be confirmed.[9] According to Bruno and his colleagues, that finding, if confirmed by further research, would further reinforce the case for investment in poor people, primarily by expanding access to education and health services as well as by the redistribution of production assets (e.g., credit and land) and the development of supportive infrastructure to small-scale rural and urban enterprises.

Overall, the essay by Bruno and his co-authors capsules much of the evidence that has broadened the scope of the new paradigm regarding growth and poverty reduction and has helped to make that paradigm more acceptable and persuasive. There is no deep or necessary tension between the macroeconomic elements of that consensus and the imperative of reducing poverty. This point has been underscored most recently in the 1997 UNDP *Human Development Report,* which states,

Careful review of evidence on income distribution and poverty available for the first time in many countries shows that in most places and times, faster growth is associated with proportional gains in income for all income groups, including the poorest. Correspondingly, during periods of economic decline, everyone loses.[10]

Moreover, UNDP perspectives on pro-poor economic measures are quite close to those of the World Bank: "job-led growth, access to credit, redistribution of land, investment in basic social services, promotion of the informal sector and sound macroeconomic policies."[11] Inasmuch as the *Human Development Report* has been highly critical in the past of growth-oriented structural reforms, this statement represents clear evidence of the newly converging perspectives on growth and poverty reduction.

There remains ample room for productive debate, and for considerable variation among countries, in the design of policies and programs that can partially buffer the poor against the costs of adjustment, enhance the effects of growth in reducing poverty, and limit the effects of transition and free markets in increasing inequality. In many developing and post-Communist countries, domestic political struggles increasingly focus on these policy choices, and on the measures needed to improve governance and build more effective public and private sector institutions to implement policies.

Reforms in these areas may prove still more controversial and politically challenging than the earlier structural adjustment or transition measures. There is only limited technical consensus on the best designs for reform in these sectors. Labor relations and social sector policies directly concern almost all of the population and engage strong emotions of fairness and entitlement. Implementing reforms in education and health is also extremely complex administratively and demands the active cooperation of all levels of government and of private as well as public sector actors and agencies. Whether and how these issues are resolved will powerfully influence both success in addressing poverty and the sustainability of the new development paradigm.

For aid donors, as well, the new pro-poor growth paradigm poses challenges for the uses of aid. Nevertheless, the challenges and arguments can now take place within a broadened consensus framework. The deep rifts of the 1970s and 1980s regarding the roles of state versus market, the choice of open versus closed growth strategies, and the primacy of growth versus poverty reduction have narrowed dramatically, even if they have not disappeared. The new statistical evidence regarding links among growth, poverty reduction, and trends in inequality provide compelling support for that narrowing of differences.

ISSUES FOR AID

■ In principle, this potential for broadened consensus on growth and anti-poverty strategies should defuse much of the debate and controversy that has surrounded the provision of development aid over the years, since that debate has really been about the strategies that aid was supposed to be supporting. Yet, while there are now the bases for more agreement on core elements of development strategy, there is also more concern about aid's effectiveness in promoting and supporting development efforts.

To a considerable extent, development assistance policies have tracked the evolution in thinking about development. In the 1950s and 1960s, development aid was viewed largely as a resource transfer needed to ease the growth-inhibiting capital constraint facing the less-developed countries. Aid was, therefore, initially provided largely in the form of large-scale financing for capital (i.e., infrastructure) investments. By the early 1970s, in the shift to a more proactive pro-poor approach to development, the targets of aid were much diversified: first to agriculture and integrated rural development; later to population, health, education, and elements of social well-being. The form, however, remained largely project financing. Then in the late 1970s and early 1980s, non-project, conditional structural adjustment lending was introduced as a major new aid instrument to promote and support the shift in focus to economic policy reform. Subsequently, with attention to additional reform problems in governance and in specific sectors, the uses of aid were further diversified.

Accompanying this evolution in development strategies and aid, there has been an accumulating body of analysis and opinion on aid's impact. The bulk of the analysis for many years focused largely on donor techniques in the design and implementation of aid projects. With the controversy that emerged over the trickle-down development strategy, critiques of aid began to focus on more profound issues of aid's broad impact on growth and development and, then, on the question of whether the aid relationship itself enhanced or impeded development prospects, and why.

For some time, aid critics from the right said that large amounts of aid going mainly to governments was having a strong disincentive effect on the development of markets and a vibrant private sector, which they saw as the only forces sure to bring efficient, sustainable development. Worse, aid was reinforcing anti-market policies, bloated bureaucracies, and inefficient public enterprises in most aid-receiving countries. At the same time, the left argued that aid policies and conditionality were promoting a kind of growth that was creating a growing gap between rich and poor; in particular, reforms proposed by the mainstream aid agencies to correct disincentives and inefficiencies were said to be increasing levels of poverty and inequality. One of the few points in common between both of these views was that aid was a powerful force—largely not to the good.

Recent measures of aid's impact on development, which tell a sobering story, challenge this basic assumption. These studies show that aid has been a less powerful force—for good or for bad—than either the left or the right previously argued. As one recent analysis says simply, aid has had no systematic effect on either growth or policy change.[12] Rather, aid is only effective in promoting growth in a good policy environment, and on the whole, it has not succeeded in leveraging good policies. The second and third essays in this volume expand on this point.

In explaining why aid has not effectively spurred policy reform—which is what the aid instrument of conditionality was precisely designed to do—studies emphasize that aid allocations by donors have not adequately rewarded good policy performance. That is, neither the rewards for good performance nor the punishments for poor performance have been strong enough to make a difference in cases of reluctant reformers. In part for political and security reasons, donors have often chosen to provide large amounts of aid to governments with little demonstrated commitment to development. Donor agencies have also been driven by internal factors—including, in the case of the international financial institutions, the need to lend "defensively" to prevent countries from falling into arrears or defaulting on their outstanding loans. This produced a tendency to create a pretense of good performance where it has not existed.[13] Where reforms have been implemented and sustained, recipient country "ownership" of the reform process—meaning involvement in the design and sustained commitment to reforms—not donor conditionality, has been key. But core features of the aid relationship have, it has been argued of late, undermined rather than enhanced that ownership.[14]

Paul Collier's essay in this volume, which focuses specifically on the failure of conditionality, concurs with this point. The essay also provides several other explanations as to why conditionality has failed to spur the policy reforms and the changes in public expenditures and investments required for growth and poverty reduction.

One of the problems with conditionality, Collier argues, is that it has tended to undermine governments' incentive to take real charge of their economies' reform. It has also made it harder for genuinely reform-minded officials to signal their true intentions to skeptical investors because their policy adjustments appeared donor-driven (and therefore not necessarily sustainable). Moreover, conditionality has made the discussion about reform one between donors and recipient governments rather than one between those governments and their publics.

Collier concludes that if aid is going to have a strong supportive effect on countries' development efforts, it must be allocated selectively to committed reformers only. His bottom line is that aid provided in a poor policy environment will do more harm than good; but aid provided in a good environment can strongly reinforce countries' growth and development potential. Moreover, highly selective aid generates additional benefits. One of these, in Collier's view, is that where selective aid promotes growth, successful "neighbors" can induce reform in other countries by being both a "role model" and a competitive "threat." A second benefit, he notes, is that this approach would turn aid flows into effective signals to private investors of governments' commitment to good policies and good governance, whereas old-style conditionality provided little encouragement to investors because it merely pointed out governments' policy incompetence and defined policy reforms that governments needed to make. Third, concentrating increasingly scarce aid funds where they could have the greatest impact could lead to more impressive outcomes from the use of donor-country taxpayers' dollars and, presumably, less objection to aid. By implication, Collier's analysis suggests that better recipient policies would ease problems of absorptive capacity, permitting strong reformers to use generous levels of aid effectively.

Others contend, however, that there are broader systemic problems with aid. One problem identified in the 1980s and given increasing attention since then has been the lack of adequate participation in the design and implementation of aid projects and programs by supposed beneficiaries. Another problem only now gaining heightened attention is said to be the high level of aid itself, especially in Sub-Saharan Africa. This is the view expressed by Elliot Berg. His essay in this volume, which provides a broader critique of aid than Collier's focused assessment of conditionality, points out that as of 1994, 27 Sub-Saharan African countries had aid-to-GDP ratios of over 15 percent and for some 20 countries the ratios was over 20 percent.

According to Berg, such high levels of aid dependence impede local commitments and ownership, and undermine institutional development and capacity building—all elements which experience has shown to be essential to development success. These unintended effects persist, in his view, not because donors lack awareness of them, but because donors and recipients cannot resolve several basic dilemmas: 1) the difficulties poor countries face in absorbing needed economic aid without suffering institutional deterioration; 2) the fact that program aid, introduced to ease absorptive problems, has tended to require more, not less, local capacity than project aid; 3) the inconsistency between donors' insistence on conditionality and their talk about the need for partnerships and local ownership; 4) the incompatibility between giving priority to donor aid agendas, including the push for quantifiable results, and the building of local ownership and capacity; and 5) the tendency of large amounts of aid, intended to promote sustainable progress, to induce a sense of resignation and passivity among national officials.

Berg's recommendations are, therefore, to apply aid not only more selectively but also in less burdensome ways. Specifically, where aid ratios are very high, Berg proposes establishing an explicit goal of reducing aid dependence over a reasonably short time even in the case of good performers. He also suggests that in making the transition to less aid dependence, donors should change the mix of aid instruments by giving greater weight to those that are institutionally unintrusive, and they should give priority to using aid in ways that build countries' capacities to design and implement their own development. Berg concludes his assessment with a recommendation for a broad-ranging dialogue between and among donor and recipient countries regarding strategies for reform coupled with reduced dependence.

KEY AID POLICY QUESTIONS

■ THE ANALYSES IN THIS VOLUME suggest a number of core questions that might usefully be put at the center of future deliberations.

1) Assuming that there is substantial agreement on the value of making aid allocations on a more selective basis, how can the development community resolve the major practical and ethical issues that a policy of selectivity would face?

What should be the criteria of selectivity? And just how selective ought donors be in drawing the line between good and bad policy performance? Is good macroeconomic performance alone enough? From the evidence it seems clear that to achieve sustainable, broad-based development, countries need to pursue sustained good macroeconomic management, pro-growth savings and investment policies, and pro-poor broad and narrowly targeted measures. All of these measures require institutional development and good governance. But is a long list of "desirables" practical?

In practice, how would judgments about performance be made? Should stakeholders and intended beneficiaries be consulted, and if so, how and when?

What does the international community do about non-performers, especially given the fact that it is the citizenry in the "non-performing" countries that suffer most? Should donors provide humanitarian and narrowly targeted pro-poor assistance even in inhospitable economic environments? If so, how much concessional aid—an increasingly scarce resource—should be used in this way? And how much should go to governments and how much to NGOs/civil society?

Can performance really hold as a basis for allocating aid? Effective selectivity depends on reasonably tight coordination among donors. This has remained for years a largely elusive aim. What is to keep donors from making aid allocations on the basis of geopolitical or commercial grounds as they have done in the past?

2) If conditionality has proved ineffective in leveraging desirable policies, how should aid be used to support the dynamics that do lead societies to choose and manage their development policies well? Collier emphasizes emulation and therefore would concentrate aid on countries whose success would stimulate others. Berg gives more emphasis to learning by doing, trial and error, and a greater focus of aid on capacity building in both government and civil society. At least by implication, Bruno and colleagues put considerable stock in the further accumulation and dissemination of compelling evidence. While these approaches are not necessarily mutually exclusive, they do suggest quite different guidelines for uses of aid.

3) Given the evidence on the importance of well-functioning institutions, what can be done about the fact that institutional development remains one of the weakest links in the aid chain? Both donors and recipients have only partial knowledge of what kinds of institutional changes should be made, very weak understanding of how those changes can be promoted, and poor experience with external efforts to help reform and build institutions.

4) How should donors and recipients think more systematically about how much aid is too much, which is Berg's concern; and how much aid is too little, which seems an implicit concern of Collier when it comes to reinforcing good performance? From these studies, it appears clear that donors have sometimes under-funded or over-funded countries. By what reckoning can the development community get a good fix on effective aid levels supportive of sustainable development efforts?

5) If the conclusion is drawn that high levels of aid dependence are themselves a problem, how can countries manage an orderly transition to less aid dependence? What would both recipient countries and donors have to do differently? How can pro-poor development strategies on which there is now wide agreement be advanced in the process?

The broadening consensus on strategies for encouraging growth and reducing poverty should provide a basis for much more cooperative and productive relations between aid donors and clients. Capitalizing on that potential, however, requires thinking through in much more operational detail the implications of the new assessments of the uses and limits of aid. The essays in this volume are presented to encourage just such a process of deliberation within and among developing countries and their aid donors.

Notes

[1] Several ODC publications during that period address this shift in approach: Robert d'A. Shaw, *Jobs and Agricultural Development*, Monograph No. 3 (1990); Robert d'A. Shaw, "Rethinking Economic Development," Development Paper No. 8 (March 1972); Robert E. Hunter, James P. Grant, and William Rich, "A New Development Strategy? Greater Equity, Faster Growth, and Smaller Families," Development Paper No. 11 (October 1972); James P. Grant, "Growth from Below: A People-Oriented Development Policy," Development Paper No. 16 (December 1973). This work continued in the 1980s with ODC's U.S.-Third World Policy Perspectives series, published in cooperation with Transaction Publishers: John P. Lewis and Valeriana Kallab, eds., *Development Strategies Reconsidered*, No. 5 (1986); John P. Lewis, ed., *Strengthening the Poor: What Have We Learned?* No. 10 (1988); and H. Jeffrey Leonard, ed., *Environment and the Poor: Development Strategies for a Common Agenda*, No. 11 (1989).

[2] World Bank, *Accelerated Development in Sub-Saharan Africa: An Agenda for Action* (Washington, DC: World Bank, 1981).

[3] Most recently, the World Bank's 1997 *World Development Report* focuses on the role of the state and the importance of institutional strengthening. Some would argue, however, that this assessment does not yet go far enough in underlining the importance of strong and effective governance. See World Bank, *World Development Report 1997* (New York: Oxford University Press, 1997).

[4] UNICEF, *Adjustment with a Human Face* (New York: Oxford University Press, 1988).

[5] World Bank, *World Development Report 1990* (New York: Oxford University Press, 1990).

[6] See Klaus Deininger and Lyn Squire, "A New Data Set Measuring Income Inequality," *The World Bank Economic Review*, Vol. 10, No. 3 (1996), pp. 565–91.

[7] In addition to the discussion of Bruno and his colleagues in this volume, see the more recent analysis by Juan Luis Londoño and Miguel Szekely, "Distributional Surprises After a Decade of Reforms: Latin America in the 1990s," Discussion Paper, Office of the Chief Economist (Washington, DC: Inter-American Development Bank, March 1997).

[8] David E. Sahn, Paul Dorosh, and Stephen Younger, "Exchange Rate, Fiscal, and Agricultural Policies in Africa: Does Adjustment Hurt the Poor?" *World Development*, Vol. 24, No. 4 (1996), pp. 719–47.

[9] Deininger and Squire, "A New Data Set Measuring Income Inequality."

[10] U.N. Development Programme (UNDP), *Human Development Report 1997* (New York: Oxford University Press, 1997), p. 72.

[11] UNDP, *Human Development Report 1997*, p. 94.

[12] C. Burnside and D. Dollar, "Aid, Policies, and Growth," Policy Research Department (Washington, DC: World Bank, 1996); and Peter Mosley, *Development Finance and Policy Reform* (New York: St. Martin's Press, 1992).

[13] Tony Killick, "Responding to the Aid Crisis," paper prepared for the G-24 Technical Meeting, March 1997, p. 2.

[14] Nicolas van de Walle and Timothy A. Johnston, *Improving Aid to Africa*, Policy Essay No. 21 (Washington, DC: ODC, 1996).

Chapter 1

Equity and Growth in Developing Countries: Old and New Perspectives on the Policy Issues[1]

Michael Bruno, Martin Ravallion, and Lyn Squire

Do the poor lose either absolutely or relatively from policies that promote aggregate economic growth? Does the answer differ between middle-income newly industrialized economies (NIEs) and low-income developing countries? These questions are not new and were very much at the center of the development debate some 20 years ago of how to achieve "redistribution with growth."[2] And yet in 1993 1.3 billion people were obliged to eke out an existence on less than a dollar a day.[3] This fact alone has led some to argue that growth-oriented reform policies of the kind usually advocated by the international financial institutions (IFIs), rather than reducing poverty, have actually worsened the lot of the poor.

This long-standing issue has recently achieved renewed prominence as many countries adjust from the growth crises of the last two decades, and as others switch from centrally planned to market-based systems. Structural adjustment programs—packages of policies designed to lay the foundation for sustained growth—have been pursued in many low-income countries and transition economies, albeit with varying degrees of intensity. Whatever the link between growth, inequality, and poverty in the long run, adjustment policies raise an additional set of questions: What are the costs to the poor during the period of adjustment? And how quickly can countries regain a high-growth trajectory?

All of these questions are important and will continue to be debated. Their resolution lies in a careful analysis of empirical evidence. In this paper, we marshall the available evidence and in particular draw on recent work that has been able to take advantage of an expanding and improved body of data.

The first section of this paper looks at long-run issues. It reviews recent evidence indicating that while income inequality differs significantly across countries, there is no discernible *systematic* impact over time of growth on inequality. Although there are exceptions, as a general rule sustained economic growth benefits all layers of society roughly in proportion to their initial levels of living. Based on the evidence of the last three decades, there seems to be no credible support for the famous Kuznets Hypothesis, which claims inequality will worsen in the early stages of development, even with rapid growth in national income. Indeed, there have been few documented cases of sustained increases in inequality in growing economies, and few cases in which the poor have failed to share in the absolute gains from higher average income.

The second section switches from long-run growth to issues of adjustment and transition. Here we argue that the key components linking growth as a necessary condition for sustained poverty reduction, and adjustment (stabilization plus structural reform) as a necessary condition for aggregate growth recovery, come out strengthened from the recent growth crises and associated reform efforts. Obviously, necessity is not sufficiency and we do not argue that growth *always* benefits the poor, or that *none* of the poor lose from any pro-growth policy reform. But we do contend that macroeconomic adjustment and structural reform are essential for sustainable growth recovery which in turn is necessary for a sustained reduction in aggregate poverty.

The first two sections of the paper support and strengthen the case for policies conducive to broad-based economic growth as part of a comprehensive poverty reduction strategy, as argued in the World Bank's 1990 *World Development Report* on poverty and the associated 1991 policy paper on *Assistance Strategies to Reduce Poverty*.[4] But a macropolicy environment conducive to growth is not enough. The second part of the poverty reduction strategy outlined in *World Development Report*, namely promoting universal access to basic education, health, and social infrastructure (as well as the adoption of social safety nets, particularly in the process of recovery from a low-level growth crisis), has in recent years received added support from new research on the *reverse linkage* from initial distribution of assets and income to subsequent growth.

The third section reviews the emerging evidence that high inequality countries, such as a number in Latin America and Africa, have lower growth and remain inegalitarian, whereas low inequality countries, such as many in East Asia, remain egalitarian and achieve rapid poverty reduction from the process of growth. The theoretical underpinnings of this reverse linkage are only gradually being understood. Some lines of argument originate from political economy considerations: concentration of wealth, such as in land or human capital, lead to policies that protect sectarian interests and impede growth for the rest of society; inequality may also enhance political instability. Another argument has to do with credit-market imperfections, whereby investment in human and physical capital is confined to the owners of initial wealth.

The final section of the paper summarizes the main conclusions and draws out implications for domestic policy and the IFIs. The most important conclusion of the paper is that policies which promote economic growth will typically also help the poor. This holds not only in the long run but also during periods of structural adjustment. A second conclusion is that countries with a more unequal distribution of assets and/or income tend to experience lower rates of growth. The important policy implication of this finding is that reducing inequality, such as through securing wide access to basic education and health, not only benefits the poor immediately but will benefit all through higher growth. This lends additional weight to the already powerful arguments for a more systematic effort to invest in poor people. The fear of a trade-off between equity and growth has been misplaced.

HOW DOES GROWTH AFFECT DISTRIBUTION?

■ IN THIS SECTION we undertake two tasks. We first examine the link between growth and inequality. If inequality worsens with growth during the early stages of development as predicted by Kuznets, then we may be confronted by a situation in which the incomes of the poor actually decline even though we observe growth in aggregate income. Since we find little support for the Kuznets Hypothesis, we turn to a second task—examination of how effective growth is in reducing poverty.

THE KUZNETS HYPOTHESIS

Recognizing that we are concerned about how the benefits of growth in aggregate incomes are distributed, the question arises as to whether there is any systematic tendency for inequality to change in the process of rising average affluence.[5] This is a long-standing issue in development economics. It is still widely held that economic growth in low-income countries will necessarily be inequitable, a view that has had considerable influence on thinking about development policy (among both advocates and critics of redistributive interventions). By this view, "the rich are usually the first to reap the benefits of national income growth."[6] Here we review the theories and evidence and provide new results on more recent and improved data.

An influential argument as to why we might expect inequitable growth in poor countries was sketched by Kuznets in 1955.[7] This claims that inequality will increase in the early stages of growth in a developing country and then after some point it will begin to fall, that is, the relationship between inequality (on the vertical axis) and average income (horizontal) will trace out an inverted U. Kuznets did not set out a formal theory of why this might happen, but sketched an argument which has subsequently been formalized. As typically presented, the Kuznets Hypothesis assumes that the economy comprises a low-inequality and low-income rural sector and a richer urban sector with higher inequality. Growth occurs by rural labor shifting to the urban sector, such that a representative slice of the rural distribution is transformed into a representative slice of the urban distribution. Thus, by assumption, distribution is unchanged *within* each sector. Starting with all the population in the rural sector, when the first worker moves to the urban sector inequality must increase. And when the last rural worker leaves, it must clearly fall again.

Between these extremes, the relationship between inequality and average income will follow an inverted U.[8]

Kuznets himself was tentative about the hypothesis. Yet it has found many supporters since, to the point of being deemed "fully confirmed" by Oshima, a "stylized fact" by Ahluwalia, and an "economic law" by Robinson.[9] Claims of support for the hypothesis can be found in a literature spanning 25 years.[10] We shall argue that the evidence presented in much of the literature is misleading because researchers have been constrained by the availability of data to conduct tests of what is essentially an intertemporal phenomenon using cross-country information. That is, variation in the level of income across countries at a point of time is being used to approximate the evolution of income through time. This implies a single relationship for all countries and thus cannot explore the more interesting question of how growth and inequality evolve within the context of specific countries. In other words, country-specific effects have been systematically omitted in much of the literature. To correct this omission, time-series data are required, which are now available. In the following section, we first assess the cross-country results and then turn to the results of recent studies using panel data and within-country time series data.

CROSS-COUNTRY STUDIES

There have been innumerable tests of the Kuznets Hypothesis on cross-country data sets. We shall not review the earlier literature here and only note that these tests have typically been ad hoc, with no clear link to the assumptions of the hypothesis. Instead, we focus on a nagging concern about all the tests using cross-country data, namely, that there may be important country-level determinants of inequality (including past inequality) which are correlated with current income levels and so lead to biased estimates. Indeed, such biases could arise solely from differences in the type of data. For example, income is a more common measure for inequality in many middle-income developing countries, notably in Latin America, whereas consumption is more common elsewhere, including among the Asian economies many of which were closer to the bottom of the income ladder 20–30 years ago when the data used to test the hypothesis were set up. And since consumption inequality is invariably lower than income inequality, these differences alone would tend to yield an inverted U relationship even if none existed using the same welfare measure. With strong latent country-level effects there can be no guarantee that differences at one point in time will reveal how inequality will evolve with growth.

If such country-level effects were not in fact a problem, then one would expect to see the inverted U reappearing in later country cross-sections. So what do data since the mid-1980s suggest about the Kuznets Hypothesis? Using data from 63 surveys spanning 1981–1992 covering 44 countries, we tried replicating a number of the specifications for testing the hypothesis typically found in the literature.[11] This was done for both levels of inequality and changes in inequality over time. In no case was there evidence of an inverted U. This also confirms earlier results for smaller samples.[12]

It appears then that the cross-country inverted U found in many earlier tests of the hypothesis mainly using compilations of distributional data for the 1950s to early 1970s may well have become blurred, if not vanished, over time. This probably reflects how various omitted variables have evolved. The new data confirm that these omitted variables were creating an appearance of a cross-country inverted U that had little to do with the hypothesis. With the growth seen in much of Asia, and the lack of it in much of Africa, the poor countries of 20–30 years ago have split into two, blurring the old inverted U but (quite possibly) better revealing the true relationship.

FURTHER INTERTEMPORAL EVIDENCE

To avoid confusing the effects of independent country-specific characteristics (initial conditions) with those of intertemporal changes of policies or economic conditions, arguments for or against the existence of a Kuznets process should ideally be based on time-series evidence. Here we report on two exercises using time-series data. The first draws on panel data covering 45 developed and developing countries for the years

1947 to 1993. It contains 486 observations on the most commonly used measure of inequality, the Gini index.[13] And the second makes use of the most extensive time-series data for any single developing country, namely India.[14]

Table 1 gives decade averages of the Gini index for each of the 45 countries for which reasonably comparable estimates are available for four or more surveys. The countries are ranked in increasing order of inequality for the 1980s, with Czechoslovakia having the most equal distribution and Brazil the least. While there is clearly variation over time (some of which could be differences between surveys and/or measurement errors), the data suggest substantially greater variation in inequality across countries at a given time than over time for a given country. Indeed fully 87 percent of the variance in Gini indices by country and date is accounted for by cross-country differences. The inequality rankings of countries are thus highly stable over the decades. The last column of Table 1 also gives the direction of the trend; a "0" in the final column indicates that there is no statistically significant trend, while a "+" indicates that inequality is increasing and a "–" that it is decreasing. Of the 45 countries covered in the data, 29 reveal no trend. And for 12 of the remaining 16 countries, the trend is quantitatively small (defined here as a change in the Gini Index of less than + or – 0.4 a year), although statistically significant.

It would not be correct to conclude from these data that distribution does not change over time. Even when there is no trend, there is variation, and seemingly small changes may matter to assessments of overall social progress, including poverty reduction (we return to this point later in the chapter). But what they do suggest is that the search for a general law linking growth and inequality must confront the fact that the vast bulk of the variation one finds is among countries, not over time. Further statistical tests on the data set confirm this point. If one allows for country-specific effects, none of the countries in the sample presented in Table 1 appear to follow the predictions of the Kuznets Hypothesis.[15]

It is worth reviewing the data for India in more detail because it is one of the most extensive and reliable series and because it bears on subsequent discussion. At the time of writing, we could construct distributions of real household consumption expenditures per person in India from 33 nationally representative and reasonably comparable household

TABLE 1. GINI INDICES, 1960–1990s (decadal averages)[a]

Country	Observations	1960s	1970s	1980s	1990s	Trend[b]
Czechoslovakia	10	22.6	20.9	21.1	.	–
Hungary	7	24.4	22.2	22.8	.	0
Bulgaria	25	22.1	21.9	23.0	27.3	0
Poland	7	.	.	25.2	.	0
Spain	6	.	.	25.7	.	0
Soviet Union	4	.	.	26.0	.	+
United Kingdom	31	25.0	24.3	27.3	32.4	+
The Netherlands	9	.	28.1	28.6	.	+
Taiwan	26	31.2	29.3	29.0	30.5	0
Finland	6	.	30.7	31.0	.	0
Norway	7	36.8	35.3	31.0	.	–
India	29	31.5	30.9	31.4	31.1	–
Canada	23	31.6	31.6	31.5	27.6	0
China	12	.	.	31.5	36.2	+
Indonesia	7	.	36.6	33.4	33.1	0
Pakistan	6	.	35.5	33.4	.	0
Italy	15	.	37.4	33.4	32.2	–
Sweden	14	.	33.1	33.7	32.3	0
New Zealand	11	.	31.4	34.1	.	+
Japan	22	35.6	34.1	34.4	35.0	0
Korea	10	31.5	36.1	35.6	.	0
Germany	6	.	36.0	35.8	45.4	+
Australia	10	32.0	36.7	36.2	32.5	0
Portugal	4	.	40.6	36.8	36.2	0
United States	45	34.6	34.5	36.9	37.9	+
Bangladesh	9	33.5	34.8	37.3	.	0
France	7	48.0	41.6	37.8	.	–
Thailand	8	42.0	41.7	37.8	.	+
Côte d' Ivoire	5	.	.	39.1	41.4	0
Belgium	8	36.4	42.0	39.6	35.8	0
Philippines	6	42.9	45.3	40.0	.	0
Singapore	6	.	39.0	40.7	.	0
Hong Kong	10	47.5	41.9	41.4	45.0	0
Venezuela	4	.	41.5	.	.	–
Trinidad and Tobago	4	.	48.5	41.7	.	0
Tunisia	5	42.3	44.0	43.0	41.0	0
Sri Lanka	7	46.0	38.8	43.7	.	0
Bahamas	11	.	48.2	44.4	43.0	–
Costa Rica	5	52.6	46.1	45.1	.	0
Malaysia	5	.	51.5	48.0	.	0
Mexico	4	55.3	49.7	.	.	–
Colombia	5	.	52.1	51.2	.	0

TABLE 1. (CONTINUED)

Country	Observations	1960s	1970s	1980s	1990s	Trend[b]
Honduras	5	.	.	54.0	52.7	0
Chile	13	.	.	54.8	53.1	0
Brazil	7	.	59.0	55.6	.	0

[a] *The table includes all countries with four or more observations, based on national household survey data. All Gini indices are measured for the same indicator (either consumption or income) over time for a given country, though it varies between countries.*

[b] *The signs indicate the trend: "–" means decreasing inequality; "+" increasing inequality; and "0" indicates no significant trend.*

Source: Klaus Deininger and Lyn Squire, "A New Data Set for Measuring Income Inequality," World Bank Economic Review, *Vol. 10 (September 1996), pp. 565–92.*

surveys spanning the period 1951 to 1992.[16] Figure 1 plots India's Gini index and net domestic product per person from 1951 to 1991. There was a trend decrease in inequality up to about the mid-1960s, but no trend in either direction after that. There is no sign that growth increased inequality, including during the period of higher growth in the 1980s. Using more formal statistical tests, one obtains, not an inverted U as predicted by Kuznets, but an ordinary U, though for most of the range of the data inequality falls as average income increases. However, if one focuses on the change in inequality rather than the level of inequality, then the relationship vanishes. There is no sign in these data that higher growth rates in India put any upward pressure on overall inequality.

OTHER LESSONS FROM TESTS OF THE KUZNETS HYPOTHESIS

The fact that there are such strong country-level effects in distribution does not mean that distribution is unchangeable. Some of the observed variation (across countries and over time) is clearly due to differences in the underlying data and measurement errors. But the literature

FIGURE 1. INEQUALITY AND AVERAGE INCOME IN INDIA, 1951–91

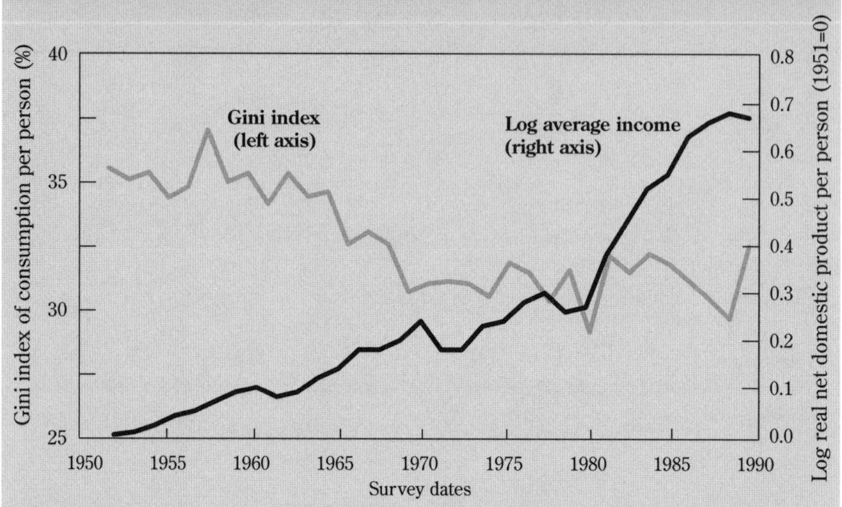

Source: Berk Özler, Gaurav Datt and Martin Ravallion, "A Database on Poverty and Growth in India," Development Research Group, World Bank, 1996.

on testing the Kuznets Hypothesis has also suggested a number of other factors which appear to influence inequality and explain at least some of the omitted country-level effects identified above. Kuznets speculates on a number of those factors, including shifting intra-sectoral inequalities, a declining share of (unequally distributed) property income, and policy changes concerning social security and employment.[17] But, on all these, the data base for testing was weak at the time Kuznets was writing. That has changed.

Higher (primary and secondary) school enrollment rates tend to be associated with lower inequality. Bourguignon and Morrisson find that a 20-percentage-point increase in the proportion of the labor force that has at least secondary education increases the share of income received by the bottom 60 percent by between 3 and 4 percentage points.[18] Papanek and Kyn find that primary and secondary school enrollment has a quantitatively important effect on the income-share received by the poorest 40 percent.[19] Human capital in primary and secondary education had a significant effect on reducing the Gini index in Korea, and increasing the share of the bottom 20 percent, whereas university education slightly increased the Gini index and did not significantly affect the bottom share of the income distribution.[20]

Mineral and agricultural exports would be expected to increase inequality to the degree that they produce concentrated rents. Bourguignon and Morrisson confirm this for developing countries where a sizable (greater than 5 percent) contribution of mineral exports to GDP was associated with a 4–6 percent decrease in the income share of the bottom 40 percent.[21] High importance (greater than 5 percent of GDP) of agricultural exports leads to greater inequality only if such exports are produced on large, rather than on small and medium farms. By contrast, Papanek and Kyn, using data for developing as well as developed countries, fail to find significant effects, presumably since failure to correct for protection does not allow inferences concerning the international competitiveness of such exports.[22] Trade theory would predict that protection lowers the reward for the most abundant (most equally distributed) factor of production and increases returns to scarce factors, which are likely to be the more inequitably distributed. There is evidence that the presence of protection worsens income distribution.[23]

Factor market distortions whereby there is a wedge between the real wage in the modern sector of the economy and the lower wage in the traditional, mainly agricultural, sector can also influence the extent of inequality. In cross-country comparisons, Bourguignon and Morrisson find that the extent of economic dualism, as measured by the labor productivity in agriculture relative to non-agricultural sectors, tends to increase overall inequality.[24]

There is also evidence for India that the sectoral composition of growth has played a role in the evolution of distribution. Recall that at the aggregate level, the data for India reveal little affect of growth on inequality. So which of the Kuznets' assumptions do not hold for India? At any one date, both mean consumption and inequality are higher in urban areas as Kuznets postulated. But the radical departure from his assumptions is in the nature of India's growth process. Growth under the Kuznets

Hypothesis is driven by rural to urban migration, assuming that the means and distributions remain the same within each sector. However, Ravallion and Datt find that this process has been only a minor source of growth in India, the bulk of which has come from intra-sectoral growth; between 1970 and 1990, the Kuznets growth process accounted for only 6 percent of total consumption growth, while growth within the urban and rural sectors accounted for 20 and 74 percent, respectively.[25]

THE IMPACT OF GROWTH ON ABSOLUTE POVERTY

The still quite widely held pessimism about the scope for reducing poverty through economic growth has rested in large part on the belief that growth would be inequitable in poor countries. We have surveyed past and new evidence on this view and rejected it as a generalization; yes, there have been cases in which growth was associated with rising inequality, but there have been at least as many cases of falling inequality. There does not appear to be any systematic tendency for distribution to improve or worsen with growth. On average then absolute poverty will fall, a conclusion that is confirmed by the results of a number of recent studies.[26]

How responsive is poverty to economic growth? Statistical analysis of 20 countries with data spanning the period 1984–1993 suggests that a 10 percent increase in the mean expenditure can be expected to result in roughly a 20 percent decrease in the proportion of people living on less than $1 per day. This reflects in part the density of people living around $1 per day. Even so, more sensitive measures of poverty—ones that tell us something about the distribution of gains among the poor—suggest an even stronger effect, indicating that the gains are not confined to those near the poverty line.[27]

Somewhat smaller effects, but broadly similar results, are obtained if we look at the evolution of poverty over 40 years in India. Using data from 33 household surveys, Ravallion and Datt find that a 10 percent increase in mean consumption would reduce the proportion of the population below India's official poverty line by about 13 percent.[28] And, as with the cross-country data, the beneficial effects of growth extend not only to those who actually cross the poverty line but also to those remaining below the line.

These results are averages. There is a variation between countries and over time in the extent to which absolute poverty measures respond to growth. Initial distribution is an important factor. Ravallion studied the effect on poverty of growth during 41 spells (made up of two comparable surveys) across 23 countries in the period 1984–1994; the results confirm that absolute poverty declines with growth, but also indicate that the responsiveness of poverty varies markedly with the degree of initial inequality.[29] In a country with a relatively equitable distribution of income (say, an initial Gini index of 25 percent), a 10 percent increase in average household income can be expected to reduce the share of the population in poverty by 33 percent. But in a country where income is initially distributed inequitably (a Gini index of say 60 percent) the same increase in income would result in only a 18 percent reduction of the proportion in poverty. This result reflects the fact that, since an increment in national income tends to be distributed in more or less the same way as existing income, the poor in inequitable societies receive only a small share of the benefits of growth.

Growth is only one of the factors that has influenced progress in reducing poverty, albeit an important one. Changes in inequality also have a strong independent explanatory power. Indeed, using the same sample we find that rates of poverty reduction are even more responsive to rates of change in inequality than to growth. Of course, changes in the level of income (growth) are much greater than observed changes in inequality. Even so, seemingly modest changes in overall inequality can entail sizable changes in the incidence of poverty. When combined with the tests of "augmented" Kuznets Hypotheses discussed above, we can postulate a number of other factors that matter through their influence on inequality, including education, the trade regime, and the sectoral composition of growth. Later we will see whether some or all of these factors might also matter to the poor via their impact on the growth process.

DO PRO-GROWTH REFORMS HAVE ADVERSE DISTRIBUTIONAL EFFECTS?

■ SO FAR WE HAVE ARGUED that the rate of overall economic growth has no systematic impact on inequality. Yet, it has been argued that some of the policy changes advocated to promote growth increase inequality.

For example, real devaluations can promote growth, but they also impact on inequality, though the direction of that effect is not obvious on *a priori* grounds. Here we look more closely at the role played by economy-wide policy changes. In particular, do the economy-wide factors (including macroeconomic policy changes) that are likely to increase the overall rate of economic growth also have distributional implications?

ADJUSTMENT AND TRANSITION

For much of the developing world, the 1980s was a period of rapidly rising servicing costs on foreign debt, external terms-of-trade shocks, and fiscal and external imbalances entailing an unsustainable excess of aggregate demand over supply. Adjustment programs were introduced to help restore macroeconomic balance, by combining fiscal contraction—cutting government spending and/or raising taxes—with supply-side measures aimed at reducing inefficiency, such as by cutting trade distortions or wasteful parastatals. Unless there is an exceptionally rapid supply-side response, somebody's consumption must fall. The distribution of the burden of adjustment has been one of the most debated issues in development studies over the last decade. The issue has been of even greater significance in the centrally planned economies that are now privatizing and placing much greater reliance on market solutions. What can we say about the impact of adjustment and transition on the poor?

Many countries were not well equipped with relevant household level data for monitoring welfare impacts of policy reform at the time that adjustment began in the early 1980s. This has since improved. Yet even with good data, it can be difficult to isolate the role played by adjustment. Poverty may have risen during an adjustment period; but it may have risen even further without adjustment. Much of the criticism of adjustment policies may have to do with the observation of real hardships that are temporarily incurred at the stabilization stage, yet would in all probability be much greater were the crisis allowed to deepen further.

One of the few clear patterns to emerge from the new household-level evidence on the evolution of poverty indicators during adjustment is that the poverty measures tend to move with the mean consumption or income of households, increasing in recession and falling in recovery.[30]

What happens to the rate of growth in the adjustment to a deep crisis is therefore crucial. In this respect, an important link to likely outcomes for the poor can be found in recent findings of relatively speedy growth recovery (in GDP though not in investment) after deep inflation (and growth) crisis.[31] The median per capita growth rate in a group of 13 successful stabilizers from more than 40 percent inflation shifted from –4 percent in the years up to and including the first year after stabilization to a positive 1.5 percent in the second year and close to 4 percent in the third and beyond.

Even when aggregate growth remains temporarily negative during stabilization, it is not at all clear which way the distributional outcome goes, as income groups whose *nominal* income is not tied to inflation, or whose income taxes are withheld at the source, will gain in relative terms as inflation falls drastically.[32] The distributional impacts of adjustment depend on the economy's initial conditions, including its openness, and the extent of flexibility in its output and factor markets. Actual experiences in distributional shifts during adjustment have been diverse. In the Philippines, adverse distributional effects resulted in higher poverty despite (modest) growth in the late 1980s.[33] A small improvement in distribution helped the poor during adjustment in Indonesia during the mid-1980s.[34] Dorosh and Sahn argue that the distributional effects of real devaluations will tend to be pro-poor in a number of African countries, since the rural poor tend to be net producers of tradables.[35] The diversity of initial conditions warns against generalizations on the distributional impacts of adjustment.

A common presumption is that countries under shock face a *dynamic trade-off*; living standards may fall in the short term during adjustment (relative to non-adjustment), but they will rise in the longer term. However, this trade-off could well be overstated. For example, Peru initially avoided adjustment, and poverty rose sharply in 1985–1990.[36] Yet the subsequent period of more orthodox reforms quickly saw positive growth and falling poverty measures in 1991–94.[37]

EVIDENCE FROM THREE REGIONS

New encouraging results have emerged for some countries in Africa. Demery and Squire use household survey data at two points of time in the mid-1980s to early 1990s to assess the change in poverty in the six African countries for which such data are available.[38] They find that the five countries experiencing improvement in an index measuring performance in fiscal, exchange rate, and monetary policies also saw poverty decline, whereas the one country in the sample that witnessed a deteriorating policy performance suffered increased poverty (Table 2).

These results cannot be extrapolated to the rest of the continent; policy implementation varied widely and on balance poverty has almost certainly increased.[39] Nor can it be concluded that all the poor benefited in the countries that saw declining poverty on average; the surveys reveal that some among the poor suffered greater deprivation. And it cannot be claimed that causality from macroeconomic policy to poverty has been established. Nevertheless, the data do confirm that improvements in macroeconomic policy are consistent with declines in poverty even in the short run. This is in turn consistent with evidence on growth; poverty fell where growth was positive and increased where growth was negative. Indeed, Demery and Squire show that the change in poverty was primarily determined by the change in mean income with changes in inequality

TABLE 2. MACROECONOMIC POLICY AND POVERTY IN AFRICA

Country	Change in Percent Poor (percent per year)	Change in Macro Policy (weighted score of macro-policy variables)
Côte d'Ivoire	+5.30	–1.65
Kenya	–0.28	+0.45
Nigeria	–1.27	+1.79
Tanzania	–1.83	+2.76
Ghana	–1.95	+1.35
Ethiopia	–3.60	+0.55

Source: Lionel Demery and Lyn Squire, "Poverty in Africa: An Emerging Picture," World Bank Research Observer, *Vol. 11 (1996), pp. 39–60.*

playing a secondary role and, at least in this sample, working in the opposite direction to growth as far as the poor are concerned.[40]

In the Latin American context, Morley has likewise demonstrated a close relationship between growth and outcomes for the poor in the adjustment process.[41] Reviewing periods of recession (falling per capita income for at least two years) and periods of recovery, he finds that poverty increased in 55 of the 58 cases of recession, and in 22 out of 32 recoveries poverty fell. Contrary to the results from the sample of six African countries where growth and changes in inequality worked in opposite directions as far as the poor were concerned, Morley finds that recessions were accompanied by rising inequality (the poor suffered doubly) while recoveries were associated with falling inequality (the poor benefited doubly). But, as in the African sample, the changes in poverty could be attributed mainly to changes in mean income.

Evidence is also now appearing for the transitional economies of Eastern Europe and the Former Soviet Union that again points to the importance of changes in aggregate GDP but also to a systematic trend toward greater inequality. As might be expected the large drops in GDP in these countries have been reflected in substantially higher levels of poverty. What is more interesting is the tendency toward greater inequality. These countries began the period with some of the lowest levels of inequality in the world. The transition has entailed consistent association between growth and inequality: Both have deteriorated.[42]

Thus we find evidence of a systematic worsening of inequality in the transitional economies as GDP has declined but observe no simple relationship between growth and inequality in the adjusting countries, although the shifts in inequality at least in Africa appear to have been larger during the adjustment phase than during periods of stable growth. We conclude from this discussion that successful adjustment usually leads to growth recovery, which will in general also reduce poverty.

Two qualifications, however, need to be made. First, it is important to stress that the detailed policy response, particularly in the *composition* of public expenditure cuts, can greatly affect the poverty outcomes of adjustment. In some cases, aggregate budget contraction has been combined with rising shares (and occasionally rising absolute levels) of public spending in the social sectors, including targeted transfers.[43] In Indonesia, the careful mix of public spending cuts during adjustment, and the rapid currency devaluations, helped mitigate the short-term consequences for the poor of declining growth.[44] Maintaining public infrastructure can also be crucial to the success of reform programs. The fiscal "crunch" often tempts governments to cut these infrastructural sectors. There is another lesson here for the nature of fiscal retrenchment during stabilization.

Second, we have said nothing about other dimensions of poverty, including human development, which may not be adequately reflected in income or consumption-based measures.[45] It is beyond our scope to go deeply into the non-income dimensions of welfare. But there is evidence to support two claims: 1) that progress in reducing income poverty is instrumentally crucial to progress against most non-income dimensions of poverty; and 2) that incomes are not all that matter, and indeed, for some non-income dimensions command over market goods may well be secondary to command over key publicly provided social services, notably access to basic health care and schooling.[46] Cuts in key categories of social spending during adjustment can entail heavy burdens on poor people, both in the short run and long run.

HOW DOES DISTRIBUTION AFFECT GROWTH?

■ So far we have looked at how growth might alter distribution. We now consider the possibility of a reverse causation. There are a number of ways in which this could happen.[47] We focus on two: credit constraints and political economy. Both have potential implications for the accumulation of capital, especially human capital, and growth. The first affects the *access* of the poor to education while the second affects incentives and the *returns* to education.

CREDIT, DISTRIBUTION, AND GROWTH

By preventing the poor from making productive investments (such as schooling), credit constraints arising from asymmetric information perpetuate a low and inequitable growth process. Furthermore, the more inequitable the initial distribution (and, hence, the greater the number of poor and typically credit-constrained people), the more severe this effect will be. A number of authors have examined credit market imperfections in general equilibrium models with lumpy investment.[48] The main result is that where credit market constraints prevent the poor from making productive indivisible investments, inequalities in the wealth distribution can have significant negative impacts on growth. What can policy do? Here we review three possible actions: provision of credit, redistribution of assets, and tax-subsidy interventions.

Intervention in credit markets aimed at channeling credit directly to rationed groups via subsidized interest rates may well reduce growth even further. In a dynamic perspective such interventions are likely to cause efficiency-decreasing distortions and rent-seeking behavior, thus further reducing growth and equity.[49]

An alternative approach entails equalizing the distribution of assets both to increase the poor's ownership of capital directly and to increase their access to credit markets. A number of analytical models have stressed the importance of the initial distribution of endowments, and the potentially large increases in social welfare that could be gained by an initial redistribution of assets.[50] Evidence from Asian countries (Japan, Taiwan, and Korea) where externally imposed land reform was followed by high growth appears to support the hypothesis. But in many situations such redistribution may be possible only with full compensation. Whether, and under what circumstances, such schemes will then pass the scrutiny of careful evaluation has yet to be determined.[51] There are often less ambitious but still potentially important opportunities for giving poor farmers greater security of tenure in places where land-rights are ill-defined.

If the informational imperfections that cause credit rationing cannot be eliminated, governments can seek ways around them by subsidizing education and taxing future wages. Assuming that higher education is reflected in higher lifetime earnings, governments can provide subsidies to schooling and finance them through a tax on future earnings, without having to deal with the problems involved in identifying individual ability.[52] It can be shown that policies mandating compulsory schooling, financed by a proportional tax on wage income, increase economic growth and, by distributing from agents with high human capital endowment to those with less, make the intragenerational distribution of income more equal.[53] Where it is very difficult to identify the "type" of individual agents ex ante, or if access to credit markets is highly unequal, such policies can be desirable.

POLITICAL ECONOMY

The preceding discussion suggests that among economies characterized by credit rationing, those with a more equal distribution of wealth will accumulate more human capital and grow faster than those marked by a more inegalitarian distribution. High inequality will also make it easier to adopt distortionary policies that will negatively affect individuals' investment decisions, stifle growth, and conceivably generate political instability.

The most common mechanism used to establish a link between political forces and economic outcomes is the notion of the *median voter*. According to this argument, the median voter's distance from the average capital endowment in the economy will increase with wealth inequality, thus leading him or her to support a capital tax rate that is higher the more unequal the distribution of wealth. This in turn would reduce incentives for investment in physical and human capital resulting in lower growth.

However, the median voter model is not a plausible description of the political process governing decision making in many developing countries. An alternative mechanism relies on lobbying. Greater wealth allows the rich to spend more resources on lobbying activities to obtain differential treatment. In the extreme form, the ability to lobby would be directly proportional to the amount of economic assets owned by an individual. A model that utilizes this assumption is provided by Persson and Tabellini who draw a connection between high concentration of land, landowners' ability to successfully lobby government for preferential tax-treatment of this asset, and the ensuing over-investment in land.[54] Such disproportionate taxation of non-landowning groups leads to increasing inequality over time and to slower growth.

Inequality of asset ownership is also at the root of the many models that relate inflation to inequality of the distribution of income. The key idea is that inflation imposes losses on certain groups and that such losses are distributed very inequitably. While inflation taxes holders of money assets, access to foreign currency and capital flight by the rich allows them to shift the burden of inflation to the poor.[55] This opens not only the possibility for the rich to park their assets abroad and then approve inflationary policies (as these would be financed by the poor), it could also form the basis for strategic behavior of the rich (in support of populist policies) that could give rise to the typical "stop-and-go" policy cycles observed in many Latin American countries.[56] Similarly, Özler and Tabellini model the "class struggle" between workers, capital, and the government; based on the capitalists' ability to invest in a risk-free foreign asset at the world interest rate, they show there is a broad range of situations where domestic investment and growth would be negatively associated with inequality in the distribution of assets.[57]

In contrast to median voter models, lobbying models can incorporate dynamic effects and strategic behavior. If politicians are self-interested, the ability of the rich to offer high bribes, and the inability of the poor to resist taxation, can lead to undesirable outcomes.[58] For example, industries affected by a negative shock may choose whether to adjust or to lobby for protection depending on the type of politician in power. Adjustment will be slower, the more responsive politicians are to lobbying, in which case growth-reducing policy interventions would be expected to increase with overall wealth inequality.

Recent models have emphasized that major policy decisions, in particular the adoption of macroeconomic stabilization measures, can be understood in the framework of a bargaining game between different social groups. While many factors beyond the distribution of income can influence bargaining power, income distribution plays an important role. Models that describe economic stabilization as a strategic game between the rich and the poor show that stabilization being associated with an increase in aggregate productivity is more likely to be delayed, the greater the inequality of the income distribution.[59] The reason is that an unequal distribution of income (or differential access to "financial technology" that could be used to diversify risk) implies that waiting reduces the utility of the rich only marginally while imposing large costs on the poor. This would, in turn, increase the probability that in the end the poor will give in and shoulder all of the cost of adjustment. The model can also be used to show that even if (often under external pressure or acute fiscal crisis) adjustment measures are adopted, the lack of social consensus or the perception by some groups that they have to pay a disproportionate share of adjustment costs may lead to backsliding as soon as the external pressures subside.[60]

THE EVIDENCE

The arguments reviewed above suggest that greater income inequality will lead to lower investment in physical and human capital and hence to slower growth. There have been a number of recent attempts to test this hypothesis. Data quality is unusually worrying here. While household survey methods have improved greatly in the last 10–15 years, a large question mark must be attached to the quality and comparability of the historical data on distribution in the 1950s, 1960s, and 1970s which have been used to test the impact of initial distribution on growth.[61] And (unlike the tests of the Kuznets Hypothesis), the noisy inequality variable is now on the *right hand side* of the regression equation, so there must be a general presumption that standard estimators will understate any adverse impact of inequality on growth.[62] While these and other issues of data and econometric specification should not be under-rated, they take us beyond our present scope.

The tests that have been reported in recent literature confirm a negative impact of initial inequality on growth, both in developed as well as developing countries.[63] For a sample of nine OECD countries, analysis of 20-year growth rates starting from 1830 show that the income share of the top quintile is negatively related to growth; it explains about 20 percent of the variance of growth rates across countries and an increase of one standard deviation in this share decreases the growth rate by half a percentage point.[64] For a sample of developing and developed countries, Clarke finds a robust relationship between initial inequality and growth that holds for different econometric specifications and independently of the regime type.[65] In addition, the empirical prediction that high inequality in landownership is associated with lower capital accumulation and growth is confirmed by Persson and Tabellini.[66] Deininger and Squire also find a significant effect in a new, and almost certainly higher quality, data set.[67] There is also evidence from a cross-section of 70 countries for the period 1960-1985 that economic inequality increases political instability and reduces physical capital investment.[68]

But the verdict is not yet in on how strong or robust the impact of initial inequality on future growth is. For example, in one test, Fishlow reports no significant effect once one controls for Latin America (with simultaneously high inequality and low growth for much of the period).[69] As in tests of the Kuznets Hypothesis, there may be some strong fixed effects in the cross-sectional relationship, though that alone does not mean the relationship is spurious like the Kuznets Hypothesis; the real test will be in how the cross-sectional relationship evolves over time. Further empirical work is needed, and the better distributional data now available should stimulate future research on this issue.

CONCLUSIONS

■ THE "STYLIZED FACT" that distribution must get worse in poor countries before it can get better turns out not to be a fact at all. Effects of growth on inequality can go either way and are contingent on a number of other factors. There is little sign in the new cross-country data we assembled of any systematic impact of growth on inequality. Possibly measurement errors are confounding the true relationship. But we think it more likely that the relationship between growth and distribution is by no means as simple as some theories in development economics have postulated. If distribution is unchanged then growth will reduce absolute poverty. Indeed, absolute poverty measures typically respond quite elastically to growth, and the benefits are certainly not, as a rule, confined to those near the poverty line.

One should be clear about what can and cannot be concluded from our results. Let us reiterate that it would not be correct to say that growth *always* benefits the poor, or that *none* of the poor lose from pro-growth policy reforms. Here we are only looking at broad aggregates. Cases of sufficiently adverse distributional impacts to wipe out the aggregate gains to the poor are unusual if not rare. But there can be large differences between countries in the extent to which growth reduces absolute poverty. The gains to poor people will tend to be lower the higher the extent of initial inequality. And even in countries with initially low inequality and a growth process which brings rapid and sizable gains to most of the poor, some will not be in a position to take advantage of the new opportunities, and some may well lose. There can be an important role here for compensatory direct interventions, providing they are well integrated into the general policy framework, in keeping with overall fiscal and monetary discipline.

Nor does the evidence suggest that growth is always distribution-neutral. Roughly half the time inequality rises, and half the time it falls. And it would also be wrong to conclude that changes in distribution are of little consequence. Indeed, we find that poverty measures respond quite elastically to changes in distribution. The point is not that distribution is irrelevant, or that it never changes, but rather that its changes are generally uncorrelated with economic growth.

While there is little convincing evidence in our view that growth tends to alter distribution in a systematic way, there are arguments as to why initial distribution matters to the nature and extent of subsequent growth. As a general rule, a more equal initial distribution will entail that a given rate of growth will be more pro-poor. It has also been argued that it will result in a higher rate of growth. This link can operate through credit market constraints, by limiting the ability of the poor to invest. The negative effect on growth is strengthened if distortionary policy interventions in favor of the rich further undermine the poor's incentives to invest. The empirical evidence on these effects is as yet mixed, though the recent literature does not support a view that higher initial inequality allows a *higher* rate of growth; some studies suggest no effect, while others suggest that high inequality inhibits growth.

Thus there does not appear to be any intrinsic overall trade-off between long-run efficiency and equity. In particular, policies aimed at facilitating accumulation of productive assets by the poor when adopted in a relatively non-distorted framework are also important instruments for achieving higher growth. The problem should not be posed as that of choosing between growth and redistribution.

When one puts these two halves together—one on the impact of growth on distribution, and the other on the reverse causation—we can begin to see the structure and some of the details of a joint model of distribution and growth, and hence of poverty. The extent to which this is a truly simultaneous model is a moot point; distribution may well affect growth more than growth affects distribution, though this interrelationship is still being researched. There is also a dynamic state-dependent structure to this joint model, in which initial conditions (of average incomes, inequality, and other factors) matter. Within this structure, a common set of policy-relevant explanatory variables can be identified, of which basic education is one of the more robust predictors of *both* variables; higher proportions of men and women with good basic schooling entails a better distribution of a larger total income.

Countries which give priority to basic human capabilities in schooling, health, and nutrition not only directly enhance well-being, but are also more likely to see improving income distributions and higher average incomes over the longer term. There are often also ways in which governments can help relieve the credit constraints facing the poor, though even means-tested credit subsidies may not be the best way; reducing transaction costs and helping people organize themselves have often proved to be better approaches. A more equitable distribution of physical assets, notably land, can also help greatly (both directly and by relieving credit constraints on investment by poor people), although the policy implications are not as straightforward as with health and education. The sectoral composition of economic growth has also been emphasized as an important factor. Sectoral biases against the rural sector in pricing, exchange rates, and public investment are not in the interests of either higher growth or better distribution. And sound macroeconomic policies appear to be essential for sustained growth, and either have no systematic effect on distribution, or have potentially adverse short-term impacts but which are typically not strong enough to outweigh the gains to the poor from growth. Paying attention to the *composition* of public expenditures in the adjustment program and to the inclusion of effective safety nets for the poor will help improve the distributional outcome in the transition to a pro-poor growth recovery.

Some of the key factors in achieving an equitable growth path, such as better schooling, also raise the current living standards of poor people, in both "income" and "non-income" dimensions. The nature of the dynamic interaction of initial conditions with future growth and distributional change can also have important policy implications. Countries with poor initial conditions (due in part to past policies) will tend to diverge from the rest. It may only be possible to overcome this if the lagging countries can get a large enough "jump start," and here there may be an especially important role for international development assistance, as private capital flows usually come in only at a later stage of the reform process. There will undoubtedly remain areas of social policy or infrastructure in which private capital will not participate even after successful reform.

The upshot of all that one knows at the present juncture is that promoting growth is good because it is a *potentially* and (in most cases) *actually* important vehicle for improving the living standards at *all* levels, and we now have a better idea about the *policies* that lead to growth, ranging from the fundamental institutional and market incentives to the promotion of macro-stability. While these policies should be pursued in all countries, we now suspect that these will be less effective in high-inequality countries: The poor benefit less from a given increment in national income in a high-inequality country, and growth tends to be lower. Thus reducing inequality is good because it will benefit the poor both immediately and in the longer term through a more pro-poor and (possibly) higher growth rate. At the same time, the political economy arguments we have advanced, caution that efforts to reduce inequality in high-inequality countries will encounter stout resistance.

These results have important implications for the changing role of the international financial institutions. Apart from the details of structural and macroeconomic policy interventions that have already been mentioned, there are two major aspects that our analysis highlights: one has to do with the *effectiveness* of foreign assistance; the other with the *externality* arising from shifts toward greater inequality.

With respect to the effectiveness of foreign assistance, it is essential in a time of declining volume of aid that each dollar is used to maximum effect in pursuit of the overarching goal of reducing poverty. Our results confirm that the IFIs should support growth-promoting policies in *all* countries. But the focus should be on countries that are clearly committed to reform and where we believe growth-promoting reforms will have the greatest positive impact on the poor. It appears that low-inequality countries may well be more likely to be responsive to the need for reforms, and more able to implement them in a shared-growth fashion. It is also the case that policies that promote growth in low-inequality countries will yield important benefits for the poor. For both reasons—commitment and impact—low-inequality countries are likely to be more effective recipients of aid. This suggests that testing commitment in high-inequality countries is especially important. Up-front actions that are both growth-promoting and equity-enhancing may be the only realistic solution but even this, experience shows, does not necessarily guarantee sustainability. Even if the agreed policies are implemented, the impact on the poor will tend to be less than in more egalitarian countries. Where up-front actions are not undertaken, donor assistance in the form of financial transfer is not likely to be effective. An important implication of this line of argument is that the aid community should adopt a strategy of greater *selectivity* among countries when allocating scarce aid resources.

With respect to the externality, an improvement in the distribution of wealth today benefits the poor directly but also benefits future generations—poor and non-poor alike—because future growth will tend to be higher through better policies and better access to credit markets. If further research establishes the strength and robustness of this result, then countries would be able to pursue redistributive policies safe in the knowledge that they also generate growth. This could be especially important in high-inequality countries. But these are precisely the countries where political power may be concentrated in the hands of those who have an interest in preserving the existing unequal distribution. The implication for the IFIs is that they should be willing to subsidize actions that encourage redistribution, especially investment in basic education and land reform.

Notes

For their helpful comments, the authors are grateful to the following discussants of the International Monetary Fund Conference on Income Distribution and Sustainable Growth: Lou Jiwei, Jacob M. Mwanza, and Dani Rodrik, as well as other conference participants, and to Klaus Deininger, Peter Lanjouw, Andrés Solimano, Jack van Holst Pellekaan, Dominique van de Walle, Holger Wolf, and Shlomo Yitzhaki. The views presented in this paper are those of the authors and should not be attributed to the World Bank.

[1] This paper, in its original form, was a product of the Office of the Vice President, Development Economics, and the Poverty and Human Resources Division and Office of the Director, Policy Research Department (Policy Research Working Paper No. 1536). It was prepared for the International Monetary Fund Conference on Income Distribution and Sustainable Growth, June 1–2, 1995.

[2] H. Chenery, M. Ahluwalia, C. Bell, J. Duloy, and R. Jolly, *Redistribution with Growth* (Oxford: Oxford University Press, 1974).

[3] The dollar a day figure is calculated at 1985 international prices using Purchasing Power Parity exchange rates. It is based on survey data for 67 countries covering 85 percent of the population of the developing world in 1990. Countries without survey data are assumed to have the same poverty rate as those with data. For details on the methodology, see Martin Ravallion and Shaohua Chen, "What Can New Survey Data Tell Us About Recent Changes in Living Standards in Developing and Transitional Economies?" *World Bank Economic Review* (May 1997).

[4] World Bank, *World Development Report 1990* (New York: Oxford University Press, 1990); and World Bank, *Assistance Strategies to Reduce Poverty*, World Bank Policy Paper (Washington, DC: World Bank, 1991).

[5] There are numerous measures of inequality that might be considered compelling, and in principle they can diverge greatly in their assessments of whether distribution has improved. In practice, however, for many of the purposes of measurement there appears to be considerable congruence among a number of these measures. We will rely heavily here on the most widely used summary statistic on distribution, namely the Gini index. This index measures inequality in a range from zero (all incomes are equal) to 100 (the richest person has all the income). There is also the question: inequality of what? Here we focus mainly on current income or consumption inequality; both may diverge from other measures that might be compelling such as inequality in life-time well-being or inequality in "capabilities" On the latter, see Amartya Sen, *Inequality Re-Examined* (Oxford: Oxford University Press, 1992).

[6] Kevin Watkins, *The OXFAM Poverty Report* (Oxford: OXFAM, 1995).

[7] Simon Kuznets, "Economic Growth and Income Inequality," *American Economic Review*, Vol. 45 (1955), pp. 1–28.

[8] For a more precise formulation and necessary and sufficient conditions for the inverted U for six possible inequality measures, see Sudhir Anand and S. M. Ravi Kanbur, "The Kuznets Process and the Inequality-Development Relationship," *Journal of Development Economics*, Vol. 40 (1993), pp. 25–52.

[9] H. Oshima, "Income Inequality and Economic Growth: The Post-War Experience of Asian Countries," *Malayan Economic Review*, Vol. 15 (1970), pp. 7–41; Montek S. Ahluwalia, "Income Distribution and Development: Some Stylized Facts," *American Economic Review Papers and Proceedings*, Vol. 66 (1976), pp. 128–35; and Sherman Robinson, "A Note on the U-Hypothesis Relating Income Inequality and Economic Development," *American Economic Review*, Vol. 66 (1976), pp. 437–40.

[10] An influential early example was in Irma Adelman and Cynthia Taft Morris, *Economic Growth and Social Equity in Developing Countries* (Stanford, CA: Stanford University Press, 1973). At the time of writing, the most recent example we know of is Rati Ram, "Economic Development and Inequality: An Overlooked Regression Constraint," *Economic Development and Cultural Change*, Vol. 3 (1995), pp. 425–34.

[11] This is the same data set used in Shaohua Chen, Gaurav Datt, and Martin Ravallion, "Is Poverty Increasing or Decreasing in the Developing World?" *Review of Income and Wealth*, Vol. 40 (1994), pp. 359–76, which gives details.

[12] See World Bank, *World Development Report 1990*; Gary Fields, "Changes in Poverty and Inequality in Developing Countries," *World Bank Research Observer*, Vol. 4 (1989), pp. 167–86; and Martin Ravallion, "Growth and Poverty: Evidence for the Developing World," *Economics Letters*, Vol. 48 (1995), pp. 411–17.

[13] For further details, see Klaus Deininger and Lyn Squire,"Measuring Income Inequality: A New Data Base," *World Bank Economic Review*, Vol. 10 (September 1996). The Gini index measures inequality in a range from 100 (perfect inequality) to zero (perfect equality).

[14] See Martin Ravallion and Gaurav Datt, "How Important to India's Poor is the Sectoral Composition of Growth?" *World Bank Economic Review*, Vol. 10 (1996), pp. 1–26.

[15] For further discussion and analysis, see Klaus Deininger and Lyn Squire, "New Ways of Looking at Old Issues: Growth and Inequality," Policy Research Department (Washington, DC: World Bank, 1996).

[16] The surveys were done by India's National Sample Survey Organization (NSO). To form the national distributions of real consumption from the NSO tabulations of nominal expenditure distributions, an allowance was made for urban-rural cost-of-living differences, and for differences in the rate of inflation between urban and rural areas. For details see Ravallion and Datt, "How Important to India's Poor."

[17] Simon Kuznets, *Modern Economic Growth* (New Haven, CT: Yale University Press, 1966).

[18] François Bourguignon and C. Morrisson, "Income Distribution, Development, and Foreign Trade: A Cross-Sectional Analysis," *European Economic Review*, Vol. 34 (1990), pp. 1113–32.

[19] Gustav Papanek and Oldrich Kyn, "The Effect on Income Distribution of Development, the Growth Rate, and Economic Strategy," *Journal of Development Economics*, Vol. 23 (1986), pp. 55–65.

[20] Jin Hwa Jung, "Personal Income Distribution in Korea, 1962–1986: A Human Capital Approach," *Journal of Asian Economics*, Vol. 3 (1992), pp. 57–72.

[21] Bourguignon and Morrisson, "Income Distribution, Development, and Foreign Trade."

[22] Papanek and Kyn, "The Effect on Income Distribution."

[23] Bourguignon and Morrisson, "Income Distribution, Development, and Foreign Trade."

[24] Bourguignon and Morrisson, "Income Distribution, Development, and Foreign Trade."

[25] Ravallion and Datt, "How Important to India's Poor."

[26] Fields, "Changes in Poverty"; World Bank, *World Development Report 1990*; Lyn Squire, "Fighting Poverty," *American Economic Review*, Vol. 83, No. 2 (1993), pp. 377–82; Ravallion, "Growth and Poverty"; Ravallion and Chen, "What Can New Survey Data Tell Us."

[27] Ravallion, "Growth and Poverty."

[28] Ravallion and Datt, "How Important to India's Poor."

[29] Martin Ravallion, "Can High Inequality Developing Countries Escape Absolute Poverty?" *Economics Letters* (forthcoming 1997).

[30] Michael Lipton and Martin Ravallion, "Poverty and Policy," in *Handbook of Development Economics,* Vol. 3, ed. Jere Behrman and T.N. Srinivasan (Amsterdam: North-Holland, 1995), Section 5.3.

[31] Michael Bruno and William Easterly, "Inflation Crises and Long-Run Growth" (Washington, DC: World Bank, 1995).

[32] This, for example, was the case for wage earners as against profit earners in the Israeli stabilization of 1985. Measurement is complicated by the fact that inflation during the household survey period will generally put an upward bias on inequality measures defined on nominal incomes; conversely, stabilization will impart a downward bias. See Nanak Kakwani, "Inequality of Income Derived from Survey Data During the Inflationary Period," *Economics Letters,* Vol. 23 (1987), pp. 387–88.

[33] Arsenio M. Balisacan, "Anatomy of Poverty During Adjustment: The Case of the Philippines," (Quezon City, The Philippines: University of the Philippines, 1993).

[34] Martin Ravallion and Monika Huppi, "Measuring Changes in Poverty: A Methodological Case Study of Indonesia During an Adjustment Period," *World Bank Economic Review,* Vol. 5 (1991), pp. 57–84.

[35] Paul A. Dorosh and David E. Sahn, "A General Equilibrium Analysis of the Effect of Macroeconomic Adjustment on Poverty in Africa," Cornell University Food and Nutrition Policy Program (Ithaca, NY: Cornell University, 1993). For a review of other recent arguments and evidence on the impacts of adjustment on the poor, see Lipton and Ravallion, "Poverty and Policy."

[36] Paul Glewwe and Gillette Hall, "Poverty, Inequality, and Living Standards During Unorthodox Adjustment: The Case of Peru," *Economic Development and Cultural Change,* Vol. 42 (1994), pp. 689–717.

[37] Edgardo Favaro and Donna MacIsaac, "Who Benefited from Peru's Reform Program?" Poverty Note 3, Latin America Country Department (Washington, DC: World Bank, 1995).

[38] Lionel Demery and Lyn Squire, "Poverty in Africa: An Emerging Picture," *World Bank Research Observer,* Vol. 11 (1996), pp. 39–60.

[39] See Chen, Datt, and Ravallion, "Is Poverty Increasing," who show that countries without adequate poverty data tend also to have worse macro performance, so compilations of available poverty data may well understate the problem.

[40] Demery and Squire, "Poverty in Africa."

[41] Samuel A. Morley, *Poverty and Inequality in Latin America: Past Evidence, Future Prospects,* Policy Essay No. 13 (Washington, DC: Overseas Development Council, 1994).

[42] Branko Milanovic, "Poverty, Inequality, and Social Policy in Transition Economies," Transition Economics Division, Research Paper No. 9 (Washington, DC: World Bank, 1995); and Ravallion and Chen, "What Can New Survey Data Tell Us."

[43] Helena Ribe, S. Carvalho, R. Liebenthal, P. Nicholas, and E. Zuckerman, "How Adjustment Programs Can Help the Poor," World Bank Discussion Paper No. 71 (Washington, DC: World Bank, 1990); World Bank, *World Development Report 1990,* Ch. 7; and Marcelo Selowsky, "Protecting Nutrition Status in Adjustment Programs: Recent World Bank Activities and Projects in Latin America," *Food and Nutrition Bulletin,* Vol. 13 (1991), pp. 293–302.

44 Erik Thorbecke, "Adjustment, Growth, and Income Distribution in Indonesia," *World Development*, Vol. 19 (1991), pp. 1594–1614.

45 Sen, *Inequality Re-Examined.*

46 On these issues, see Sudhir Anand and Martin Ravallion, "Human Development in Poor Countries: On the Role of Private Incomes and Public Services," *Journal of Economic Perspectives*, Vol. 7 (1993), pp. 133–50; and Benu Bidani and Martin Ravallion, "Decomposing Social Indicators Using Distributional Data," *Journal of Econometrics*, Vol. 77 (1997), pp. 125–40.

47 Quite generally, when markets are incomplete there will be efficiency implications of changes in distribution: See Karla Hoff, "The Second Theorem of the Second Beast," Journal of Public Economics, Vol. 45 (1994), pp. 223–42. Some specific examples in the literature are reviewed in Lipton and Ravallion, "Poverty and Policy," Section 5.1.

48 Abhijit V. Banerjee and Andrew F. Newman, "Occupational Choice and the Process of Development," *Journal of Political Economy*, Vol. 101 (1993), pp. 274–99; Daniel Tsiddon, "A Moral Hazard Trap to Growth," *International Economic Review*, Vol. 33 (1992), pp. 299–321; Gilles Saint-Paul and Thierry Verdier, "Historical Accidents and the Persistence of Distributional Conflicts," *Journal of the Japanese and International Economies*, Vol. 6 (1992), pp. 406–22; Oded Galor and Joseph Zeira, "Income Distribution and Macroeconomics," *Review of Economic Studies*, Vol. 60 (1993), pp. 35–52.

49 Valerie Bencivenga and Bruce Smith, "Financial Intermediation and Endogenous Growth," *Review of Economic Studies*, Vol. 58 (1991), pp. 195–209.

50 Banerjee and Newman, "Occupational Choice"; and S. Chatterjee, "The Effect of Transitional Dynamics on the Distribution of Wealth in a Neoclassical Capital Accumulation Model," Working Paper (Philadelphia: Federal Reserve Bank of Philadelphia, 1991).

51 Ongoing World Bank involvement in market-assisted land reform operations in South Africa and Colombia would provide an opportunity to test this empirically.

52 Karla Hoff and Andrew B. Lyon, "Non-Leaky Buckets: Optimal Redistributive Taxation and Agency Costs," NBER Working Paper Series No. 4652 (Cambridge, MA: National Bureau of Economic Research, 1994).

53 Zvi Eckstein and Itzhak Zilcha, "The Effects of Compulsory Schooling on Growth Income Distribution and Welfare," *Journal of Public Economics*, Vol. 54 (1994), pp. 339–59.

54 Torsten Persson and Guido Tabellini, "Is Inequality Harmful for Growth?" *American Economic Review*, Vol. 84 (1995), pp. 411–17.

55 Saint-Paul and Verdier, "Historical Accidents."

56 Raul Laban and Federico Sturzenegger, "La Economia Politica De Los Programas De Estabilizacion," *Coleccion Estudios CIEPLAN*, No. 36 (December 1992), pp. 41–66.

57 S. Özler and G. Tabellini, "External Debt and Political Instability," NBER Working Paper No. 3772 (Cambridge, MA: National Bureau of Economic Research, 1991).

58 S. Lael Brainard and Thierry Verdier, "Lobbying and Adjustment in Declining Industries," *European Economic Review*, Vol. 38 (1994), pp. 586–95.

59 Alberto Alesina and Allan Drazen, "Why Are Stabilizations Delayed?" *The American Economic Review*, Vol. 81 (1991), pp. 1170–88.

[60] Laban and Sturzenegger, "La Economia Politica."

[61] Some of the "data points" in these older compilations were not even based on household surveys but were synthetic estimates, and the quality of the survey data sets used was highly variable; for an overview of these issues, see Fields, "Changes in Poverty." Recent compilations have gone some way toward eliminating these problems; see Chen et al., "Is Poverty Increasing or Decreasing?"; Deininger and Squire, "Measuring Income Inequality"; and Ravallion and Chen, "What Can New Survey Data Tell Us."

[62] This arises from the usual "attenuation bias" in ordinary least squares regressions when there is random measurement error in the right hand side variable. Additionally, there is likely to be an "aggregation bias" in standard tests using country or regional data; see Martin Ravallion, "Does Aggregation Hide the Harmful Effects of Inequality on Growth?" Development Research Group (Washington, DC: World Bank, 1997).

[63] Alberto Alesina and Dani Rodrik, "Distributive Politics and Economic Growth," *Quarterly Journal of Economics*, Vol. 108 (1994), pp. 465–90; Persson and Tabellini, "Is Inequality Harmful for Growth?"; George R. G. Clarke, "More Evidence on Income Distribution and Growth," *Journal of Development Economics*, Vol. 47 (1995), pp. 403–28.

[64] Persson and Tabellini, "Is Inequality Harmful for Growth?"

[65] Clarke, "More Evidence on Income Distribution."

[66] Deininger and Squire, "Measuring Income Inequality."

[67] Persson and Tabellini, "Is Inequality Harmful for Growth?"

[68] Alberto Alesina and Roberto Perotti, "Income Distribution, Political Stability, and Investment," NBER Working Paper Series No. 4486 (Cambridge, MA: National Bureau of Economic Research, 1993).

[69] Albert Fishlow, "Inequality, Poverty, and Growth: Where Do We Stand?" in *Annual World Bank Conference on Development Economics 1995*, ed. Michael Bruno and Boris Pleskovic (Washington, DC: World Bank, 1996). However, Clarke reports that the inequality effect on growth is robust to this and other changes in specification. See Clarke, "More Evidence on Income Distribution."

Chapter 2

The Failure of Conditionality[1]

Paul Collier

Conditionality has failed. Most of Africa does not have even minimally adequate economic policies and where such policies are in place investors fear reversal. Africa is rated as the most risky investment environment in the world. This essay argues that this has arisen from major mistakes in the design of the aid relationship. First, it reviews what aid has achieved to date. The disturbing new evidence is that aid has achieved little despite a scale of resource transfer which is in itself remarkable. Next the essay presents a diagnosis of why the aid "instrument"—conditionality intended to induce African governments to reform policies—has been misguided. The discussion then moves from critique to alternative proposal. The aid relationship has so evidently failed to deliver acceptable performance that a critique is almost otiose. However, the message of this essay is not that the aid budget should be slashed to make way for whatever else is on the wish-list, but that easily implemented design changes could make aid dollars a high priority with Western electorates. No one who has seen African poverty can honestly say that the West cannot *afford* to do anything about it. No one who has seen the evidence on aid effectiveness can honestly say that aid is currently achieving its objective.

The Western development profession has largely reacted to this conundrum by claiming that African development is complex. On the contrary, this essay argues that the answer to African aid ineffectiveness is remarkably simple.

WHAT HAS AID ACHIEVED TO DATE?

■ TO THE EXTENT THAT AID is justified by the benefits to the recipient, rather than to the lender, it might reasonably be judged on three criteria: growth, poverty-alleviating public expenditures, and policy reform. The evidence indicates that aid has largely failed on each of these criteria.

Recently there have been two well-conducted econometric studies of the relationship between aid and growth. The first study, by Boone, concluded that there was no relationship: Aid went into consumption and so provided no impetus to the growth process.[2] The second study, by Burnside and Dollar, came to a more nuanced and indeed more credible conclusion. It found that the impact of aid depended upon the policy environment. In good policy environments, aid enhanced growth; in sufficiently poor policy environments, it actually reduced growth. Over a wide range of intermediate policies, they concluded, like Boone, that it had no effect.[3] Clearly, the key issue for developing countries turns on what is meant by good and bad policy environments. Burnside and Dollar defined these in terms of macroeconomic and resource allocation variables such as the fiscal deficit and the parallel exchange rate premium. In Africa, which is the focus of this paper, Burnside and Dollar had a sample of 23 countries, 15 of which were classified as having policies sufficiently poor that growth would be reduced by aid. It therefore seems reasonable to conclude that in most of Africa to date, aid has not augmented growth and may indeed have contributed to the unusually low rates of growth that Africa has experienced since the mid-1970s.

Even if there is no effect upon growth, aid may nevertheless be justified if it alleviates poverty by augmenting public expenditures. This is, after all, the main rationale for providing most aid in the form of projects rather than as generalized budget or balance-of-payments support. It has long been recognized that aid is "fungible" to an extent. Aid given for one purpose can end up financing something else, because in the absence of aid, the government would have financed the project itself. However, new evidence by Feyzioglu and his colleagues reveals that the extent of fungibility is greater than previously imagined.[4] With the exception of transport projects, which are often so large that governments could not otherwise finance them, aid is totally fungible. There is no relationship between the composition of project aid and the composition of the budget. An extra dollar of project aid on social expenditures produces no greater increase in the social expenditure budget than does an extra dollar of free, unrestricted resources to the government. This is not to say that the linking of aid to projects is useless. There may well be a transfer of technical knowledge about projects as a result of the need to formulate and negotiate specific projects to secure aid. However, it does mean that project aid is quite ineffective in changing the composition of government budgets.

While aid is almost entirely fungible within the government budget, Feyzioglu and his colleagues find that an extra dollar of aid increases public expenditure by at least a dollar and indeed by somewhat more than a dollar.[5] In the language of the World Bank, aid does not reduce "tax effort." In less loaded language, this means that the government is not transferring any of the aid to private agents except by means of its own augmented expenditures, which are in turn unrelated to the projects agreed with donors. This is not necessarily something about which donors should be pleased. Typically, African governments spend around a fifth of GDP. There is some presumption that as in developed countries the share of government in GDP reflects an approximation of balance achieved through the political process between the costs and benefits of public and private expenditures. Even if this is only approximate, it seems unlikely that whereas on average only a fifth of resources are channelled through the government, it is appropriate to channel 100 percent or more of aid resources through government expenditure. Some degree of passing aid on to the private sector by means of tax reductions is probably an efficient use of aid. The marginal dollar of tax revenue imposes both collection and disincentive costs, so that a dollar of aid spent on reduced taxation confers benefits on the private sector well in excess of one dollar.

It is indeed possible that aid has increased rather than reduced taxation because of the donor emphasis on tax effort. For example, in Uganda the donors have insisted that the government raise its tax revenue by one percentage point of GDP per year. The rationale for this has been that Uganda should avoid aid dependency by building its revenues quickly to the point that they can finance expenditure. Although this rationale sounds sensible, it is in fact both ludicrous and self-defeating. Such carelessness in argument could only survive in a shallow intellectual environment such as has characterized thinking on aid. I will now justify these severe remarks.

A country such as Uganda, which is extremely poor by any standards but has an unusually good policy environment, will be a recipient of aid for many years even in the best of circumstances. As long as the Ugandan policy environment continues to be satisfactory, it is scarcely conceivable that within the next decade an increasingly rich West will decide that it cannot afford to finance Ugandan development. However, for the sake of argument, suppose that the donors really are going to "taper" aid, removing it over the course of the next decade. The attempt to force up revenue to GDP ahead of this tapering has the opposite effect to the fiscal sustainability which donors seek. By insisting on rising tax revenue at a time when aid itself is rising, the donors are leaving the Ugandan government with only three options in how to use the aid. The first, and most likely, is that government expenditure will rise. This is indeed consistent with the evidence of Feyzioglu and his colleagues discussed above: A dollar of aid increases government expenditure by more than a dollar because it is successfully conditioned upon increased tax revenue. Far from achieving sustainability, this pushes government expenditure as a share of GDP to a level that is unsustainable without aid and indeed pushes taxation to a level that would not have otherwise been chosen. Around the world, government expenditures are subject to a ratchet effect: Once increased they prove very difficult to reduce. Hence, the donor-induced increase in government expenditures is building a future scenario of post-aid fiscal crisis.

A second use of aid is to accumulate reserves, which is barely a use at all because the aid does not augment the real resources flowing into the country. Already countries such as Uganda have reserve levels relative to their imports more that double those of prudently managed Western economies such as Germany. Donors surely do not intend their aid to be used in this way. Further, the accumulation of large reserves itself increases the danger that the government will succumb to populist, fiscally irresponsible policies. For example, one interpretation of Nkruma's ruination of Ghana is that he inherited very large gold reserves that tempted him into unsustainable expenditures.

The third and most sophisticated use of aid is that the government will run a fiscal surplus with the banking system. In effect, the government would lend to the private sector via the banks. This is the policy of "tax and lend." The government taxes the private sector and lends the money back to it. The problem with a tax and lend strategy is that in the African context it is likely to be extremely inefficient. The taxes raised impose high distortionary costs at the margin, while the banking system is too weak and inexperienced to lend effectively.

The Government of Uganda has used the revenue from its increased tax effort for each of these purposes: Expenditure, reserves, and the surplus with the banking system have all risen. Yet the costs of increased revenue have been highly visible. The government has few viable "tax handles" on the economy, and so in practice it has raised revenue by import duties and by very high taxes on gasoline. One of the best-established relationships in development is that impediments to trade retard growth, and so there is good reason to believe that the import duties have had this effect. The high taxes on gasoline are probably even more detrimental. Ugandan gasoline prices are more than double those in neighboring countries. The incidence of these taxes probably falls disproportionately on the rural population since gasoline is an important input into rural-urban transport costs, which in turn increase the costs to the rural population of transacting in the market as opposed to surviving by means of subsistence. Yet in Uganda, where the rural population retreated into subsistence during the Amin period, the essence of the development process is this reintegration to the market. Indeed, the high gasoline tax in Uganda is leading to increased smuggling as traders gradually learn to evade the tax.

An implication is that by retarding the growth process and inducing evasion, high taxation is delaying the buildup of the taxable base of the economy and so is delaying the time at which fiscal sustainability can be achieved. An efficient "turnpike" to sustainability would involve using aid to finance a phase of low taxation, enabling the most rapid accumulation of subsequently taxable activities. There would be no need for donors to insist upon tax effort. Once aid actually started to taper off, the government would be faced with a choice between higher taxes or reduced expenditure. As noted above, governments around the world faced with this choice have implemented higher taxes.

One reason why donors have insisted upon increased tax effort as a condition for aid is that they have quite inappropriately transferred the intellectual underpinnings of household-level workfare programs to the domain of governments, assuming that just as welfare households are work-shy so African governments are tax-shy. However, African governments have not been tax-shy. On the contrary, they raise revenues from fees and export taxes despite popular discontent. Rather, they are expenditure-insensitive, allowing public money to be wasted. For example, the President of Uganda had to campaign for votes but once to discover that there was overwhelming pressure to eliminate primary school fees. A tracking survey of government expenditure on primary schools found that aside from teachers' salaries, only 37 percent of the money released from the Ministry of Finance actually reached primary schools, the rest getting diverted into administrative expenses along the way. It is thus a gross misreading of the political economy of African government behavior for donors to press for yet higher taxation, while, as has been seen above, having no effective means of influencing even the broad composition of expenditure, let alone its detailed efficiency of execution. If anything, donors should be attempting to restrain governments from raising taxation. The incentive argument analogous to the underpinnings of workfare is actually that African households are being discouraged from exporting and investing by the high taxes which governments impose.

I now turn to the third criterion on which aid might be judged, namely policy reform. Aid might be entirely spent on useless government consumption and yet be remarkably effective if it induces governments to adopt growth-inducing and poverty-reducing policies. This is indeed the core of what conditionality is supposedly about—aid buys reform. Unfortunately, it does no such thing.

Two World Bank studies find this apparently remarkable result. The first, *Adjustment in Africa: Reform, Results, and the Road Ahead,* in its final appendix table classified 26 African countries according to whether policies had improved or worsened and whether aid had increased or reduced. The table showed that whereas in most aid-increasing countries policies had worsened, in a large majority of aid-reducing countries, policy had improved.[6] More recently Burnside and Dollar have found that econometrically there is no relationship from aid flows to policy change: Aid has simply not bought reform.[7] Some governments have chosen to reform, others to regress, but these choices appear to have been largely independent of the aid relationship. The micro-evidence for this result has been accumulating for some years. It has been suppressed by an unholy alliance of the donors and their critics. Obviously, the donors did not wish to admit that their conditionality was a charade. Equally, the critics of market-friendly policy reforms—largely Marxist academics and the nongovernmental organization (NGO) community—wanted to attribute the impetus to reform to imperialist donors rather than to African governments. Donors and their critics thus connived at exaggerating the power of donor conditionality out of proportion to its true effects.

Had conditionality been effective in inducing policy reform, Africa would now have growth-friendly policies. This, however, is far from the case. To illustrate this point, I pass low-income African countries across three low hurdles, each fairly uncontroversial as a necessary condition for rapid growth. (Some 8 percent of the African population lives in middle-income countries, but for this discussion, I focus only on low-income countries.)

The first hurdle is that governments should provide a minimum level of social order. During the 1990s, 11 percent of the African population has been living in civil war environments. Economic statistics are a casualty of such conditions so the growth rate of this group of economies is not known, but more general evidence on the effects of civil war suggest that per capita incomes will have been falling at around 4 percent per year.[8]

The next hurdle is a minimum degree of macroeconomic order. I avoid controversially low inflation thresholds and apply the test of inflation below 25 percent on average over a three-year period. During the 1990s, an astonishing 45 percent of the African population has lived in environments where there is peace but not macroeconomic stability. Again recent economic data are a casualty, but per capita incomes have also been falling for this group as far as we can tell.

The remaining hurdle is more complex, namely the avoidance of very poor resource allocation policies. I utilize an unpublished World Bank assessment of five aspects of resource allocation and consider governments to have met this hurdle if they avoid the worst rating for each of these policies. A further 12 percent of the African population live in environments which although peaceful and macroeconomically stable have very poor resource allocation policies. For this group the economic statistics are better and per capita incomes have been falling. This leaves 23 percent of the African population in low-income countries in which governments are providing what I would describe as the "minimum adequate economic environment." Many of the countries in this group have only just arrived there. For example, those countries which belong to the Franc Zone had an overvalued exchange rate and therefore poor resource allocation policies until 1994. During 1994 and 1995, the per capita GDP of this group grew at an annual rate of just over 3 percent. While this is not spectacularly fast, the policy environment which I have delineated is not spectacularly good. However, it suggests that even in only somewhat stable environments, Africans can achieve respectable growth rates. The recent evidence on performance thus contains a double message. First, despite a decade of conditionality—and an aid flow estimated at $64 billion under the Special Program of Assistance for Africa—African governments have largely failed to deliver even a minimum adequate economic environment. Second, in the minority of countries in which such an environment has been achieved, the growth response is quite encouraging. The core failure of conditionality is not, therefore, that it has been pressing for the wrong policies, but that it has failed to achieve them.

WHY HAS CONDITIONALITY FAILED?

■ SOMETHING HAS EVIDENTLY BEEN SERIOUSLY WRONG with conditionality. Most dramatically, the traditional instrument of donors, project lending, was so flawed that it failed to influence the composition of government spending. Further, as the World Bank has come to realize, the rate of return upon projects has been highly dependent upon the policy environment.[9] The solution to the project lending problem was adjustment lending. As we have seen, this failed to achieve its objective of policy reform and I now consider why.

First, except in the short term, government policy is determined by domestic political forces. In Africa prior to democratization, the powerful constituency was essentially urban. Bates identified the coalition that ruled the typical African state as having an interest in high agricultural taxation and high public sector employment.[10] The offer of aid for reform can temporarily disturb this political equilibrium but is unlikely to change it. For example, Morrisson and his colleagues show econometrically how the political response to reforms has typically been urban protest followed by government policy relapse.[11] In effect, they show that the equilibrium identified by Bates is locally stable in response to aid-induced policy disturbances. This is not to say that Africa is locked into unreformed economic policies. On the contrary, there have been some remarkable policy reforms in the last half-decade. However, the impetus for this has been a mixture of democratization, past failure, the collapse of the control-regime models of development, and the growing success of the open-economy role models.

Until very recently with the honorable new models of South Africa and Eritrea, African governments almost never declined aid-for-reform packages, even if they had little intention of sustaining the reforms. African governments simply did not regard donor threats as credible. Some donors were motivated by political considerations. Others became locked into defensive lending, needing to lend more and encouraging others to lend to service their original loans. The purchase of policy reform became little more than a charade for packaging these defensive aid flows.

The weakness of the link from government policy implementation to aid flows has now been established econometrically, again by Burnside and Dollar.[12] Aid flows predominantly to low-income countries, as is surely appropriate, but within this group there is very little selectivity. Disaggregating by type of donor, the international financial institutions apply limited selectivity; the bilaterals virtually none. One reason for this, which came to be regarded as *the* conditionality problem within the World Bank, was what might be regarded as the "nuclear deterrent dilemma." Because many reforms, often 60 or more, were packaged into a single reform agreement and subjected to the same conditionality, a failure to implement any one of the reforms on schedule, for whatever reason, technically constituted a breach of the agreement for which the penalty was program suspension. But program suspension would plunge the country into default on its debt service and so trigger a crisis in the country and visible failure for the Bank and Fund staff responsible for the country. Donors generally felt that this was an inappropriately severe penalty for often minor breaches. Lacking lesser penalties, they therefore waived the conditions. Consider, for example, the astonishing story of relations between the Government of Kenya and the World Bank. During a 15-year period, the Government of Kenya sold the same agricultural reform to the World Bank *four times*, each time reversing it after receipt of the aid. Faced with such behavior on the part of the donors, it would have required an astonishingly credulous government to take notice of donor conditions. In the language of economics, the aid-for-reform packages were "time inconsistent," facing governments with different incentives before and after the receipt of aid.

One consequence of this unhappy state of affairs was that it became much harder for the genuine reformers among African governments to signal their true intentions. The appearance of conditionality was that all reforms were done at the behest of the donors against the wishes of African governments. The true reformers, who stuck to the reforms, were thus cast more as poodles atypically incapable of standing up to the donors, rather than as the courageous pioneers they in fact were. For example, Uganda is now recognized as an outstanding African success, but the credit for its tight budget is claimed by the International Monetary Fund (IMF). Meanwhile the Zimbabwean fiscal collapse is celebrated in denunciations of the IMF by Zimbabwean President Mugabe. Conditionality has thus had the inadvertent outcome of enabling African governments only to signal their policy incompetence. Failures are clearly attributable to governments; successes are not.

This inability of reforming African governments to signal their true intentions has been very damaging. Survey evidence of potential investors to Africa during the 1990s has shown that the single major impediment to investment has been the fear of policy reversal. Risk raters, such as Institutional Investor and Euromoney, rate Africa as the riskiest continent. Indeed, there is evidence that they rate it even more severely than is warranted by the fundamentals. New research at the IMF finds that although risk ratings in regressions are largely explicable in terms of measurable aspects of past performance, Africa is systematically rated worse than is justified.[13] Similarly, in a new study of foreign direct investment (FDI), the International Finance Corporation finds that investment to Africa is inexplicably low. They conclude,

> This gives some support to the conjecture that investors may be irrationally averse to committing FDI to African countries since the Africa effect appears to dominate a range of fundamental economic, political, and social risk factors in the regression analysis.[14]

Since revival of private investment is probably the key to achieving rapid growth in Africa, the perverse effects of conditionality on the signaling capabilities of African governments should be regarded as serious.

By the mid-1990s, the deficiencies of the massive reform packages had become apparent to the donors and a new style of program lending emerged. This took the form of "short-leash" lending in which individual reforms were priced. Staying with the nuclear deterrent analogy, this can be thought of as the doctrine of flexible response. Such a program would take the form of a menu of desired reforms composed by the donors, each with a price tag attached, in which governments chose which reforms they would sell at which time. Donors would pay on delivery, a feature known technically in aid jargon as single tranche operations, by which is meant that there is no payment in advance of implementation. This gets round the problem of the nuclear deterrent and reduces the problem of unimplemented promises. However, it leaves other problems as severe as ever and introduces new ones.

First, it does not address the problem of Kenya-type behavior in which the government actually implements the reform but subsequently reverses it. There is nothing in single tranche lending to prevent the same reform being put on the menu year after year, with the government selling the reform repeatedly.

Second, it is still premised on the "social costs of adjustment" mentality, in which aid compensates governments and their citizens for the short-term costs of abandoning poor policies. The whole notion of such costs has been hugely exaggerated. At the aggregate level, major economic reforms usually increase growth almost at once. For example, trade and exchange rate liberalizations, the centerpiece of the African liberalizations, usually raise output even in the first two years of their implementation.[15] At the level of individual households, the notion that poor households are the ones hurt by reform is usually false.[16] Although some households lose, they tend to be the better-off ones, such as the beneficiaries of privileged access to imports and civil servants. Only where both the formal and informal market economies have been demolished by the control regime is there a serious poverty problem associated with transition, such as has been experienced in the formerly communist economies of Eastern Europe. In Africa such economies are rare, but they experience the same problems (for example, Guinea).

By framing the rationale for program aid in terms of the imagined costs of adjustment, donors contribute to an environment in which governments exaggerate the costs of policy reform. If each reform is priced and sold to donors with an underlying rationale of compensation for costs, then the preference of the government must be to maximize the unit price of each reform by dwelling on its costliness. If a government genuinely wished to reform—and would do so without aid because it believed the costs to be trivial relative to the benefits—it would have severe difficulties in justifying an aid program, if it behaved honestly within this mental framework. A disturbingly close analogy to the piecemeal pricing of reforms is the productivity deals between unions and employers that were required to justify wage increases during the British Incomes Policy of the 1970s. Although this was intended to speed productivity growth, it had precisely the opposite effect. Unions instructed the workforce not to implement any change in work practices unless it had been sold to management as part of a productivity deal, and indeed workforces reinvented arcane work practices to sell their subsequent removal.

More fundamentally, the pricing of reform is diametrically opposed to ownership of the reform process by the government. Yet all parties now accept that a reform program can only be credible if the government sees the reforms as its chosen course of action. The very language of the pricing of reform should indicate its conflict with ownership: If donors price reforms, they buy them and governments sell them. Who then owns the reforms? An extreme instance of this was when President Moi of Kenya became irritated with the insistence by Western governments on civil rights. In response, he threatened *to reverse the reform program* if the Western governments did not stop pushing the civil rights issue. This revealed quite clearly who was regarded as owning the Kenyan reform program; the statement only made sense if all concerned saw ownership as residing with the donors rather than with the government.

There is a further, more technical, but highly important problem with designing program aid as a flow of purchases of reforms. The resulting flow of aid is likely to be highly volatile and so give rise to macroeconomic instability because whereas the *social* costs of adjustment have received far more attention than is warranted, the *political* costs have become much more important as a result of African democratization. Most of the African population now lives under governments that are sufficiently democratic to subject themselves to contested elections, typically every five years. Although this is recent in Africa, we can infer its consequences for policy reform from what has happened elsewhere in the world, namely the "political business cycle." Around the world, governments are fiscally more lax and less inclined to implement unpopular policy changes in the two years before an election. A corollary of this is that the "shadow price" of policy change rises sharply as the government approaches an election, and the rate of sales of reforms would consequently diminish. The macroeconomic repercussion of this political behavior is that aid flows would be strongly cyclical, which is highly inefficient. An aid program should be a source of stability to an otherwise shock-prone economy, not itself the source of crisis.

A NEW BASIS FOR CONDITIONALITY

THE FLOW OF AID SHOULD REFLECT—and be conditioned on—the level of the policy environment, not the flow of reforms. According to the results of Burnside and Dollar, aid enhances growth in good policy environments and retards growth in bad policy environments. The effectiveness of aid does not depend on the pace of policy reform but on the level which policy has reached. Nor is there evidence that aid, by attempting to buy reform, can significantly accelerate the pace of reform. Thus, conditionality should be used not to induce policy change but to ensure that aid goes to environments where it can be effective.

SELECTIVITY VERSUS INCENTIVES

Ensuring that aid goes to good policy environments can be termed *selectivity*. Donors set conditions that identify environments where aid will enhance growth and alleviate poverty. This can be contrasted with the current use of aid—as *incentive* for policy change. With selectivity as the criterion, aid flows to good policy environments identified on the basis of actual achievements; with incentives as the criterion, aid flows to bad policy environments in which the government promises to implement reforms. Hence, selectivity is based upon retrospective assessments of performance and so is *ex post,* whereas incentives are based on promises and so are *ex ante*. The criterion of incentives skews aid toward the worst policy environments because it is these environments in which there is most scope for promises of policy improvement. Selectivity and incentives are alternatives as criteria for conditionality (that is, using aid as an incentive has an opportunity cost in that it cannot be used for selectivity).

The main reason for preferring selectivity over incentives is that it would radically improve aid effectiveness measured in terms of impact upon growth and poverty reduction. Aid has failed to buy reform, and it is ineffective except in good policy environments. Thus, if aid continues to be used to induce reform in poor policy environments, it will continue to be ineffective. As this becomes recognized, the whole political basis for aid will be undermined and resource flows will be curtailed. In a rich, fast-growing, and peaceful developed world, the abandonment of the poor would be repugnant. The impulse for charity is in general income-elastic: Aid flows might be expected to increase even more rapidly than developed country incomes and to concentrate on a diminishing group of poor countries.

That this is not currently happening is a measure of how discredited aid has become with developed country electorates. Enhanced aid effectiveness is essential for recovery of aid flows. At present, poor countries with good policy environments are losing heavily because of the failure to direct aid to them. Resources that would work in their environments are being wasted in other environments. As a result of the waste of aid, overall aid budgets are already much lower than they would otherwise have been. In turn, the donor community has become so pessimistic about the future that continued aid flows are regarded as highly uncertain. Medium-term planning is thus conducted on the assumption that aid will drastically diminish. For example, the present fiscal planning projection for Uganda foresees aid diminishing to only around one percent of GDP over the next eight years. The average African country has in the past decade received around ten percent of GDP as aid. Uganda has one of the best policy environments in Africa and one of the very lowest incomes in the world. If the Ugandan government maintains the policy environment, the developed world should pour aid into Uganda for the next two or three decades, which is the horizon over which rapid growth could lift the population out of poverty. That planners of the Ugandan economy are seriously contemplating a medium-term scenario in which aid will evaporate is a measure of how costly the aid pessimism engendered by aid ineffectiveness has become.

A second reason for preferring selectivity over incentives as the criterion for aid is that selectivity will probably be more effective in inducing reform in poor policy environments. Donors and international financial institutions (IFIs) have hugely exaggerated their power to influence policy in African environments. Chronically bad governments, such as that of Mobutu in Zaire, have been manifestly impervious to donor influence. Even moderately poor governments, such as that of Moi in Kenya, have taken the measure of the donors and decided that they can work the time inconsistency feature of the aid game rather than undertake sustained reforms. Only a combination of informed and empowered wider domestic constituencies and the presence of successful neighbors will induce reform in these countries. The effect of neighbors should not be underestimated.

A neighbor with a good policy environment, and consequently a rapidly growing economy, is a major stimulus for change—partly as a role model and partly as a potential threat. For example, when the new government came to power in Tanzania, it inherited a poor policy environment and a slow-growing economy. One of its first actions was to invite in leaders of the Ugandan policy and business communities to learn how Uganda had built an environment in which the economy was growing at around 10 percent per year. Similarly, the collapse of the Mobutu regime demonstrates that governments which produce disastrous policy environments cannot defend themselves against the conjunction of internal dissent and more successful neighbors. Outside of Africa, the East Asian miracle has surely been reinforced by both the role model and the threat effects of neighbors. If emulation of neighbors is the main motor by which good policies will spread across Africa, then the pace of emulation will depend on a phase of strong differentiation. That is, Africa needs a few spectacularly successful countries that become the envy of their neighbors. The role of the donors in this process is thus to accentuate the effects of policy differences by concentrating aid in the good policy environments.

It might seem that this is a harsh and regressive strategy, but it is not. The countries with good policy environments happen to be disproportionately drawn from the lowest income countries. This is not a matter of chance; a common antecedent of sustained reform is a prolonged phase of major policy error, which both provides a learning experience for the economy and impoverishes it. Hence, targeting aid to good policy environments does not mean neglecting the poor. On the contrary, it would focus aid more strongly on poor countries. It would, however, acknowledge the limits of donor power. Aid agencies are not a substitute for a government and cannot save the local population from a bad government. The local population has to save itself through political action. Through contributing to the success of neighbors, however, donors can provide the populations of poorly governed countries with the evidence that refutes government excuses for failure.

So far I have compared the present use of conditionality as an incentive with a proposed use for selectivity. There are three other uses of conditionality that are also useful to this discussion: *paternalism*, *restraint*, and *signaling*.

PATERNALISM

Paternalism in this context is the attempt by donors to impose their own preferences on how aid is spent by a government. This is a perfectly legitimate use of conditionality. The condition might stipulate, for instance, that the money should be used for child immunizations rather than for the extension of the presidential palace. Donors currently adopt paternalism along with incentives as the basis for conditionality. There are, however, problems with using conditionality in this way. One is that paternalism conflicts with incentives. If the president really wants to extend his palace while caring little about child health then the lure of aid as an incentive for him to reform policies will be less effective if the aid cannot be spent on what he wants. Since I regard the use of aid as an incentive for policy reform as misguided, I do not see this in itself as a very serious problem, though it is one for those who would defend the present basis for conditionality.

A more important problem is that paternalism has simply been ineffective. Recall that Feyzioglu and his colleagues find no effect of the composition of project aid on the composition of government expenditure. Governments behave as though aid were free resources in their budgets even though donors attempt to be highly paternalistic in directing how aid should be spent. If donors have been unable to implement paternalism in the past, they are unlikely to be able to implement it in the future because various changes have made their task even harder.

One change is that democratization has reduced the legitimacy of paternalism. Donors have less basis for overriding the preferences of a government when that government has been elected to a term of office and a program of policy than when it has no legitimacy. Donors should hesitate before overruling democratic governments having recently pressed so strongly for democracy.

A second change is that many African governments are decentralizing budgetary decisions to local levels, again often with the support of donors. Yet decentralization, by design, disempowers the central government from budgetary allocation, and donors have no institutional capacity to replicate conditionality negotiations at the local political level. (In some countries this would mean 30 or 40 local negotiations.)

Third, paternalism creates a signaling problem between governments and their electorates somewhat analogous to the effect of incentive conditionality on the signaling of a government to investors. If donors claim the credit for all the projects with high social impact, such as schools and clinics, festooning buildings and vehicles with their advertisements as is common, then electorates lose faith in governments and begin viewing their own taxes as pure predation. Donors should leave governments the space in which to look good with their electorates by means of service delivery attributable to themselves.

Finally, and most important, governments need to take responsibility for the *design* of service delivery programs. In much of Africa, the provision of basic public services is a chaotic amalgam of the distinctively designed projects of a multiplicity of donors. Each donor promotes its own design, partly to support the consultancy services of its own country. This produces complex programs that could not be mastered even by a highly sophisticated civil service, let alone the weakly staffed services of Africa. Donors should get out of the business of designing and selling projects to governments. Where governments lack the skills internally to plan programs, they can commission external technical assistance. The model for aid would thus be one in which governments designed or chose programs, and donors would then choose between governments to find environments in which aid would be most effective in achieving their objectives. The pertinent features of the environment would include both broad economic policies, such as exchange rate and trade regimes, and the design and competence of service delivery. Donors would thus take account of the environment in making their choices but would not directly intervene in attempting to alter that environment. Donors have had over 30 years to make intervention work and have failed to do so.

RESTRAINT

A further objective of conditionality is *restraint*—a mechanism whereby the government is discouraged from certain policies. In the African context, restraint is very important. Recall that Africa is rated as the riskiest region in the world by investors and that the fear of policy reversal is reported by them to be the single biggest impediment to investment. A shrewd reforming government will choose to lock itself in to its reforms to the extent possible by constructing a variety of restraint mechanisms. By restricting its possible actions, a shrewd government excludes those policies which it would not in fact wish to choose, but which, while they exist as options, reduce the effectiveness of the policies the government does implement. Thus, paradoxically, by introducing restraints on itself that do not in fact change its behavior because they restrain only actions it does not wish to do, a government is able to relax constraints that really are binding, such as limited investment. Some of these restraint mechanisms are domestic; some are external. For example, cash budgets and independent central banks are attempts by the government to create domestic agencies of restraint. The binding of tariffs within the World Trade Organization is an example of using an external agency of restraint. Conditionality can be an external agency of restraint and indeed has been so used for the past decade. However, the very poor risk ratings of Africa are testimony to the perceived ineffectiveness of conditionality as a restraint. It has failed as a credible restraint for two reasons.

First, as discussed above, conditionality has been overburdened with a myriad of detailed points of policy change. Typically, a government signing a structural adjustment loan will be committing itself to around 60 promises of policy change. What is reassuring to investors is not these promises of policy change but commitments to the maintenance of perhaps two or three fundamental aspects of the policy environment, such as convertibility of the currency and a degree of fiscal prudence. Thus, conditionality as a restraint has been devalued through over-use. It is an instance of the more general exaggeration of donor power.

Second, part of the point of a restraint mechanism is that it is in the interest of a good government and so will be chosen by it. Just as a shrewd government chooses to bind itself by means of a cash budget, so it will choose to bind itself through conditionality. However, it will do this very selectively. Western governments hardly ever bind themselves with respect to promises of making policy change because the future is too uncertain and reneging on commitments uses up credibility. No Western government would dream of committing itself to 60 specific policy changes over a two-year period. Governments can only reasonably be expected to commit to the maintenance of policies. There is indeed little point in commitments to future policy change: The strongest commitment is less convincing than the act of actually implementing the change. Policy changes that can be implemented rapidly might as well just be implemented because pre-commitment adds no value. With policy changes that are complex and need a long time to implement, the credibility of pre-commitment is likely to be limited. Because each failed pre-commitment burns up the overall credibility of the government, the costs of such promises are likely to outweigh the benefits.

With respect to donor conditionality, the key credibility problem is the donors' record of forgiving breaches of conditions. This can only be overcome by increasing the moral legitimacy of donor punishment of breaches of conditions, and the most effective way of increasing moral legitimacy is if the conditions are very few and are volunteered by the government. By making conditionality voluntary, the donors would transform the moral space in which negotiations are conducted. The language of partnership, so fashionable with donors, would be transformed from hypocrisy to reality. Shrewd governments that wanted to build credibility would opt for conditions; crooked, populist, and stupid governments would avoid them; and investors would draw conclusions from this behavior. Governments and donors would be cooperating to enhance the investment environment.

SIGNALING

The final role for conditional aid is as a *signal*, providing information to private agents. This is an enormously important and unexploited use of the aid relationship. The private sector, especially investors in developed countries, are largely ignorant of African opportunities. Private capital flows to developing countries could potentially swamp public capital flows. Further, dollar for dollar, private investment is probably more effective in growth and poverty alleviation than aid. A major objective of aid then should be to assist the inflow of private capital to Africa. Private investors lack information about Africa because until recently returns on investment were low. A recent estimate of average returns on investment over the period 1960–1990 finds that they were one-third lower in Africa than in other developing countries.[17] Indeed, Africans themselves have moved their portfolios abroad. It is estimated that by 1992 around 70 percent of African private wealth (excluding land) was held outside Africa.[18] With the improvement in the African policy environment, however, this has changed. During the 1990s, the returns on FDI have been around 60 percent higher in Africa than in other developing regions.[19] Because most investors have not done business in Africa and perceive it as a difficult investment environment, they seldom put Africa on the shortlist for investment locations. They therefore never acquire the information necessary for an informed decision and so face threshold costs of information which act as a deterrent to investment. Potentially, investors can substitute for the lack of direct information by using the commercially available risk ratings, but as mentioned above, these ratings are systematically biased against Africa. Risk ratings do respond to changes in the policy environment, but only with a long lag time. Thus, after ten years of sustained reform, Uganda is still rated as the eighth most risky country in Africa, approximately the same as Nigeria.

The IFIs have an enormous informational advantage with respect to Africa. They have large teams of highly qualified staff with full access to both data and policy employed on each country. Private rating agencies and international investors have nothing remotely comparable. Yet at present the information flow from the IFIs to the private sector is very limited. Even were this rectified, the most credible basis by which private investors can act on Bank-Fund information is to infer their true opinions from their actions. Potentially, a Bank-Fund lending program to a country should signal to investors that that country is a good policy environment, but at present this does not appear to be the case. Rodrik finds that international private capital flows to a country are actually reduced by a Bank-Fund program. Investors appear to treat it as a signal of distress rather than as an assurance of quality control in economic policy.[20] Investors would not have been very wrong with such an interpretation. The imperative of defensive lending has often directed programs to crisis economies rather than to those with good policy environments. Were conditional aid to be based upon the criterion of *ex post* selectivity rather than incentives-cum-paternalism-cum-defensive lending, then aid flows would signal a good policy environment and thus investment opportunities. Aid would then be in a position to lead private capital flows instead of deter them.

In addition to turning aid flows into an effective signal for private investors, the shift to *ex post* selectivity would enhance the ability of governments to signal to investors. Recall that a consequence of the detailed, *ex ante* conditionality practiced to date is that when governments adopt good policies, the attribution is claimed by the Fund and Bank and so cannot be interpreted as the free choice of the government. With *ex post* selectivity, donors would come in behind reforms rather than anticipating them. For the early stages of reforms, perhaps the first three years, the government would be reforming without aid, establishing a good policy environment. Governments which reformed in this way would unequivocally establish with investors that they were reforming because they believed that the reforms were needed. They would also have to justify the policy changes to their domestic populations in terms of their underlying sense rather than in terms of donor conditions.

Examples of this approach to reform are rare because Bank and Fund programs have anticipated reforms. Due to a legal anomaly, however, there is one clear case, namely Vietnam. When Vietnam embarked upon its reform program in 1991, the United States was still maintaining its embargo on lending to it and was able to prevent lending by the IFIs. The embargo was not lifted until four years into the reform program. Despite the absence of donor funding, the Government of Vietnam successfully implemented a reform program and is now attracting private capital inflows on a scale far beyond that realized in Africa. It is an open question to what extent these capital inflows are induced by Vietnam's location in East Asia, and to what extent they are due to the credibility achieved through reform clearly attributable to the intentions of the government. However, Vietnam demonstrates that it is entirely possible to reform an initially highly controlled economy without aid, and its experience is at least consistent with the hypothesis that such a reform attracts private capital more rapidly because of enhanced credibility. In Africa, a somewhat analogous but more recent example of reform without adjustment lending is South Africa. To date, there has been a large private capital inflow to South Africa, again consistent with the hypothesis of enhanced credibility.

TRADE-OFFS AND CHOICES

To summarize, I have contrasted five criteria for conditionality and shown that the criterion of incentives conflicts with its use for any of the other four. Selectivity would focus aid on already reformed policy environments instead of attempting to buy reform in bad policy environments. Effective restraint would focus conditions on the maintenance of a few core policies which would be voluntarily specified by governments, instead of attempting to specify future policy changes in detail. Effective signaling to investors would require aid flows to reflect established good policy environments rather than hopes of improvement in bad ones and would require governments to be given enough freedom over policies that the adoption of good policies was clearly attributable to governments. Even paternalism conflicts with the use of aid as an incentive for policy reform because it reduces the value of aid to the government.

Faced with a conflict between objectives, economists naturally think in terms of a trade-off. The use of aid as an incentive has an opportunity cost in terms of the other objectives and so must be traded off against them. In this trade-off, what donors choose depends in particular upon the elasticity of policy with respect to aid. If policy were highly elastic with respect to aid then, in effect, the pace of policy reform would have to be traded off against the effectiveness of aid for given policies. Selectivity would give the best impact of aid for given policies, whereas incentives would give the best impact of aid on policy. Conversely, if the elasticity of policy with respect to aid were zero, there would be no trade-off between the pace of policy reform and the effectiveness of aid for given policies. Selectivity would have no opportunity cost in terms of policy impact. At present the best research estimate is that the elasticity of policy with respect to aid is indeed zero. Further advances in research may well produce a more nuanced result, showing that in some political environments aid might assist policy reform whereas in others it retards it. However, at present there are no such results and what is clear is that the policy impact of aid is far less than had been envisaged when the instrument of conditionality was designed. Thus, the choice on the trade-off between incentives and the other uses of conditionality should unambiguously shift away from incentives. My own view is that the incentives objective should be abandoned altogether. Aid should simply flow into those low-income countries with already good policy environments. This would enable the levels of aid to these countries to be increased substantially. In turn, since we know that aid is effective in raising the growth rate in good policy environments, this aid would produce some dramatic African successes, probably with growth rates in excess of ten percent per year. At such growth rates, GDP will double in less than seven years, and I would expect that within this time scale the effect of emulation would have transformed a large group of African policy environments. However, I would accept that my own position is not the only one which is sustainable on the evidence. Some continued incentive role for conditionality may be justifiable. What seems incontrovertible is that this is considerably less than has been the practice to date.

In this essay, I have not considered how *ex post* evaluations of performance as the basis for selectivity should be conducted, although I have done so elsewhere.[21] I suspect that there is a broad consensus on what constitutes satisfactory performance, but there is more disagreement on the difference between satisfactory and good policies than between satisfactory and unsatisfactory performance. My own preference for performance criteria is that they should be based on the African average, which implicitly builds in peer group pressure and enhances legitimacy in the process. If a government is failing to deliver the African average, it is reasonable to ask why. This criterion can be nuanced by allowing for many country-specific features, but the goal is a criterion that would attract broad consensus *within Africa*. Legitimacy is not only desirable in itself, it is necessary to reestablish the credibility of conditionality, and with it, the credibility of the African policy environment.

CONCLUSION

■ DURING THE LAST DECADE, donors have coordinated on a massive and in its way remarkable transformation of the aid relationship. Some $64 billion has been directed to Africa under the auspices of the Special Program of Assistance, under which donors have presented a coordinated face to African governments, offering aid in return for policy reform. The fruits of this relationship have been meager relative to the resources involved. During this same period, African performance on average deteriorated both absolutely and relative to other developing areas.

I have suggested that this poor performance is attributable to fundamental design failures in the conditionality relationship. Governments have been lured into promises on policy change that no Western government would dream of making. The resulting broken promises have undermined the already limited credibility of African governments. Even those few governments that have complied with the conditions can be seen by potential investors not as being committed to reform, but as poodles of the international institutions. More fundamentally, aid has simply failed to induce policy change. The attempt to do so has resulted in aid being wasted in policy environments where it cannot be effective.

In place of using conditionality to induce policy change, I have proposed that it should be used to reward those governments with established good policy environments, a strategy I have termed *selectivity.* This includes some of the poorest countries in Africa, so the change of strategy would not involve a regressive redistribution to richer countries. Further, by creating star performers, selectivity would induce many nonreforming governments to change their policies through the pressures of emulation. Selectivity would make aid dramatically more effective. This would both produce a larger reduction in poverty per dollar of aid and rehabilitate aid in the currently jaundiced eyes of Western electorates. On the day that I write this conclusion the Burnside and Dollar results have been written up in the *Financial Times*. It emphasizes that on average aid has failed to achieve any impact on growth but notes that in good policy environments aid augments growth. As this message get popularized and quite possibly distorted, the aid industry has only a short time to reform itself before politicians respond to popular disillusionment. At present, about a quarter of the African population is living in low-income environments in which aid can be effective in alleviating a poverty so shocking that when ordinary people in developed countries are physically confronted with it they are often traumatized. These ordinary people have never been so well off, nor have they ever had such a secure future of rising prosperity in the context of global peace. If aid budgets continue to fall in this context, the aid industry will have itself to blame—but the price will be paid by the African poor.

Notes

[1] This essay draws heavily on joint work with Jan Willem Gunning. Intellectually, it should be considered as joint work, although readers familiar with that work may detect a falling off from our usual standards of literacy.

[2] P. Boone, "The Impact of Foreign Aid on Savings and Growth" (London: London School of Economics, 1995).

[3] C. Burnside and D. Dollar, "Aid, Policies, and Growth," Policy Research Department (Washington, DC: World Bank, 1997).

[4] T. Feyzioglu, V. Swaroop, and M. Zhu, "Foreign Aid's Impact on Public Spending," Policy Research Department (Washington, DC: World Bank, 1996).

[5] Feyzioglu, Swaroop, and Zhu, "Foreign Aid's Impact on Public Spending."

[6] World Bank, *Adjustment in Africa: Reform, Results, and the Road Ahead,* World Bank Policy Research Report (New York: Oxford University Press, 1994), Table A27.

[7] Burnside and Dollar, "Aid, Policies, and Growth."

[8] P. Collier, "The Economic Consequences of Civil War" (Oxford, UK: Centre for the Study of African Economies, 1996).

[9] J. Isham and D. Kaufmann, "The Forgotten Rationale for Policy Reform: The Productivity of Investment Projects," Policy Research Working Paper No. 1549 (Washington, DC: World Bank, 1995.

[10] R.H. Bates, *Markets and States in Tropical Africa* (Berkeley, CA: University of California Press, 1981).

[11] C. Morrisson, J.-D. Lafay, and S. Dessus, "Adjustment Programs and Politico-Economic Interactions in Developing Countries: Lessons from an Empirical Analysis of Africa in the 1980s," in *From Adjustment to Development in Africa,* ed. G.A. Cornia and G.K. Helleiner (London: Macmillan, 1994).

[12] Burnside and Dollar, "Aid, Policies, and Growth."

[13] N.U. Haque, M. Nelson, and D.T. Mathieson, "Creditworthiness Ratings: Their Political and Economic Content," in *Risk and Agencies of Restraint: Reducing the Risks of African Investment,* ed. P. Collier and C. Pattillo (London: Macmillan, 1997).

[14] F. Z. Jaspersen, A.H. Aylward, and A.D. Knox, "The Effects of Risk on Private Investment: Africa Compared with Other Developing Areas," in *Risk and Agencies of Restraint: Reducing the Risks of African Investment,* ed. P. Collier and C. Pattillo (London: Macmillan, 1997).

[15] J.D. Sachs and M. Warner, "Economic Reform and the Process of Global Integration," *Brookings Papers on Economic Activity,* No. 1 (Washington, DC: The Brookings Institution, 1995), pp. 1–118.

[16] D. E. Sahn (ed.), *Economic Reform and the Poor in Africa* (Oxford: Clarendon Press, 1996).

[17] P. Collier and J.W. Gunning, "Explaining African Economic Performance," Working Paper WPS97-2 (Oxford, UK: Centre for the Study of African Economies, 1997).

[18] P. Collier, A. Hoeffler, and C. Pattillo, "The Portfolio Choices of Nations" (Oxford, UK: Centre for the Study of African Economies, 1997).

[19] A. Bhattacharya, P.J. Montiel, and S. Sharma, "Private Capital Flows to Sub-Saharan Africa: An Overview of Trends and Determinants," Research Department (Washington, DC: International Monetary Fund, 1996).

[20] D. Rodrik, "Why Is There Multilateral Lending?" in *Annual Bank Conference on Development Economics 1995*, ed. J.M. Bruno and B. Pleskovitc (Washington, DC: World Bank, 1996), pp. 167–93.

[21] P. Collier, P. Guillaumont, S. Guillaumont, and J.W. Gunning, "Redesigning Conditionality," *World Development* (forthcoming September 1997).

Chapter 3

Dilemmas in Donor Aid Strategies[1]

Elliot Berg

A growing consensus has emerged in recent years among donors, and between aid agencies and their developing country counterparts, on development strategies. Almost everybody now agrees that sustainable development requires macroeconomic stability, substantial integration into the global economy (which implies adequate export performance and competitive markets), more effective public sector management, more effective poverty alleviation, and greater attention to the private sector and to civil society in general.

The substantive consensus is much more robust on the general level than in the details. Differences persist on numerous matters, such as the scope to be allowed the private sector, the role of foreign investment, the speed and sequencing of movement to competitive markets, and the relative weight to be given to direct attacks on poverty. Debate on the role of the state remains particularly lively, much of it framed in terms of the exportability of the East Asian experience. Whether, how, and to whom state enterprises should be privatized is a related area of controversy. The applicability of some specific policy instruments remains in contention—market-based interest rates, devaluation, and input subsidies for farmers, among many others.

Though by no means trivial, these questions of substance are now of much less significance than issues of process, issues that involve the nature of the aid relationship itself. It has become increasingly apparent that in many countries, particularly the least developed that are the most heavily aided, much has gone awry. The aid process itself has revealed features that dilute its medium-term effectiveness—notably by impeding local commitment and ownership. It also has unintended negative longer-term effects—the undermining of institutional development and capacity building. These process-related problems are the focus of this chapter.[2]

Most of the problems at issue are well known. Observers and practitioners have long deplored the absorption of key local officials in meetings with aid missions and in related travel. They have pointed out the management burdens arising from varied and complex donor administrative, accounting, and monitoring requirements. And in even more fundamental matters, they have noted the donor-driven character of aid projects and weak local commitment to donor-sponsored policy reform programs.

Donors have tried to come to grips with these issues. For years, virtually every review of aid effectiveness and related strategy statements have hammered on the point that success and sustainability of development programs or policy reforms depend strongly on local commitment, which requires local ownership. All donors have been preoccupied with introducing more partnership, more local participation, transparency, and genuine dialogue. It is the same with capacity building. Donor policy statements have elevated the nurturing of local capabilities to the front rank in priority.

Nonetheless, in the low-income countries that now are at the center of aid donor concerns, not much partnership is observable on the ground. And although greater attention is certainly being given to capacity building, results are not yet evident in most of these countries. Many donor approaches and policies continue to discourage the growth of both local capacity and local ownership. This is what casual observation suggests, but there is other evidence. The results of formal opinion surveys in Sub-Saharan Africa (for example, World Bank borrower surveys) indicate that ownership of numerous policy reform programs and projects remains weak.

The unintended negative effects found in so many heavily aided countries persist not because of donor lack of awareness or lack of conviction that they should be eliminated. Rather, they persist because of inability to resolve some basic dilemmas. Donors and their developing country partners have not yet faced the full implications of these contradictions and the tradeoffs in objectives that they require.

CONTRADICTIONS IN THE AID PROCESS

■ THE FOCUS IS ON FIVE of these contradictions. Although they are most relevant to the least developed, most heavily aided countries, they also apply to aid relationships in general.

■ ***The poorest countries have the greatest need for economic assistance but are least able to absorb it without suffering institutional deterioration.***

Low-income countries with few exceptions have weak public administration. They have low-paid and usually demoralized civil services, poorly functioning budgetary systems, and unsystematic decision-making processes. Their ability to formulate, implement, and evaluate policies and reform programs is slender. Project-making capacity is usually only slightly stronger. Ability to coordinate policies and programs is almost everywhere embryonic.

Foreign assistance in such circumstances is bound to have institutionally unsettling effects, even if the aid is limited in scale and well conceived in substance. Aid management—receiving aid missions, negotiating agreements, coordinating aid programs with domestic programs and policies, meeting the diverse and burdensome reporting and accounting requirements of the different donor agencies, ironing out the numerous little bumps that typically arise in implementation of these programs—can and often does absorb the attention of a high proportion of key officials in poor countries with thin administrative systems.

This is true even where aid inflows are small relative to the size of the recipient economy. Negative institutional effects escalate as aid becomes more important. For countries where aid inflows are relatively large—say 5 percent of GDP—these effects are unsettling; at higher aid levels, they become devastating. At aid-to-GDP ratios of 10 percent or more, aid accounts for rarely less than half of public investment. Counterpart funds generated by program assistance finance a substantial share of domestic expenditures. Aid projects finance many of the vehicles and most of the copiers and other minor equipment in the public sector. Strategic recurrent costs are picked up by donors to keep projects operating.

Aided governments in these circumstances lose command over most of the functions that are central to development. They control investment expenditure in only the loosest way; donors not only finance but also design, implement, and evaluate most projects, with varying but usually minor local participation. Policy reforms are crafted elsewhere; local inputs are reactive at best. Even domestic financing is strongly influenced by rules for access to counterpart funds, at least where program assistance is substantial. Control of salary and manpower policy is eroded as donors hire local staff for "their" projects or contract with them to meet donor needs. Dual salary and incentive structures undermine morale and commitment among public sector employees who are left out of donor-distributed assignments. And, finally, donors until recently set up autonomous project units and coordinating entities to fill unmet or bypass inefficient (sometimes corrupt) government bodies. This neglect or subversion of existing structures creates organizational confusion and contributes to the withering of government capacity.

These tendencies to administrative decline are most observable in the heavily aided countries, the bulk of which are in Sub-Saharan Africa. Thus since 1975 net annual official development assistance (ODA) has rarely been less than 5 percent of GDP in any African country; for the region as a whole (excluding Nigeria and South Africa) it averaged 6 percent in 1975-84, 9 percent in 1985-89, and nearly 13 percent in 1990–94.[3] In 1994, this country average was almost 16 percent. Of the 44 Sub-Saharan countries for which numbers are at hand, the ODA-to-GDP ratio exceeded 15 percent in 27 countries, and it was greater than 20 percent in 20 countries. Outside of Africa, high ODA-to-GDP ratios are found in Bangladesh and Laos; less striking but still substantial ratios exist elsewhere.

The point here is that most of the unintended negative consequences of the aid presence do not flow from poor donor country policies or heavy-handed bureaucracy. Undoubtedly, the adoption of more flexible and enlightened donor policies and practices could mitigate some of these unwanted effects. But, however reformed and enlightened, the maintenance of such high levels of assistance will continue to overwhelm local administrations and impact perversely on local ability to manage resources.

■ ***Comprehensive or sectoral programming requires more—not less—local capacity.***

In part to deal with the absorptive capacity constraint in aided countries, multilateral and bilateral donors alike have advocated replacement of the present "project-by-project approach" with a "program approach." One of the main advantages claimed for this change is that it will make it easier for local governments to manage aid. Just what a program approach means is not always clear and varies between donors. A good general statement is in a 1991 report of the Development Assistance Committee of the Organization for Economic Cooperation and Development (OECD):

> The programme approach should be based on thematic, sector-wide, multidisciplinary, and often multi-donor actions. . . . [Aid agencies have agreed that they] will plan and manage . . . aid increasingly in the context of coordinated support for larger sectoral programmes, objectives, and policies.[4]

The European Union (EU), many bilaterals, and other multilaterals have expressed agreement with this general orientation.[5] But each donor gives it a different spin. Thus the United Nations Development Programme initially concentrated on better and more complete programming of technical assistance through its National Technical Cooperation Assessment Programme (NatCAP). It has more recently promoted truly comprehensive country programming exercises that would include all ODA. The World Bank is advocating "integrated sectoral investment programs" that aim to incorporate under local management all projects in a sector, however financed.

A sector programming approach might make aid coordination easier, and it might also reduce some local administrative burdens through scale economies. It also has other potential advantages; it could, for example, result in a sharpening of sector policy objectives and closer links between policies, projects, and programs.

By themselves, however, programming approaches do little to increase the aid absorptive capacity of local governments. Programs cannot be built on sand. They are built on projects, those basic units of action that have a starting and finishing date, specify output targets, and indicate what it will take in physical inputs and money to achieve those targets. With or without broader programming, the need to identify, cost, appraise, and screen projects remains. To move toward programming without sound underlying projects is to risk a loosening of priorities and a reduction in the effectiveness of development spending.

Programming then, does not do away with the need for good projects. At the same time, it demands additional capacity for framing sectoral policies and putting together projects into integrated programs. Only if programming is accompanied by other steps that directly reduce local management burdens—notably by simplifying, harmonizing, or reducing their accounting and administrative requirements for disbursement—will the absorptive capacity constraint be loosened.

■ ***Donors can not continue to talk about partnership and the urgent need to enhance local ownership while pushing conditionality.***

The rationale for conditionality is well established. It can strengthen the hand of local reformers against bureaucratic and political opponents of reform. It is said to be essential to prevent recipient governments from using (highly fungible) program assistance simply to finance their budget and external payments imbalances, without making essential macroeconomic policy adjustments. When donor and client governments have different sets of priorities, conditionality is needed to prevent reallocation in favor of local priorities. It also may be aimed at preventing more crudely illegitimate use of donor resources. And in any event, conditionality is necessary to reassure donor country legislatures and the governing bodies of international financial institutions that aid money is not being wasted.

Whatever the strength of these arguments, it has to be recognized that the imposition of conditionality has costs as well as benefits.

One of the costs is the risk that game-playing will ensue. Both parties have an interest in keeping the agreements on track and tend therefore to minimize risks of nonperformance. Faced with weak compliance and reluctant to impose sanctions, donors tend to stretch definitions of acceptable performance.

These behaviors were common in the initial phases of policy-based lending, especially structural adjustment lending. They are perhaps less common and less subversive in the mid-1990s. The greatest problem now with conditionality is its fundamental incompatibility with genuine dialogue and hence joint problem-solving and the growth of local ownership.

Donors may seek ways around this uncomfortable reality by broader use of prior actions and by more persistent consultation at the policy and program formulation stage—for example, by giving responsibility for first draft as of key documents to local governments. Such steps alleviate but do not remove the problem.

First, even where local technocrats and their ministerial allies are unconvinced that policy orientations are right, there is little propensity to wander from conventional paths. Policy frameworks are established, usually by International Monetary Fund (IMF)–World Bank staff, and these pretty much define what is to be done and not done. The process is sometimes facilitated by donor provision of consultants to assist in producing the requisite policy documents. It is no surprise that some cynics speak of "ventriloquism" in these arrangements.

Second, conditionality is profoundly at odds with open debate in recipient countries. In many developing countries, and probably in most of the least developed, the conditionalities in policy loans are not known by the general public. In many—probably most—cases, even fairly senior officials do not know the specifics. This alone is hard to reconcile with the more open and democratic styles of governance that have emerged in recent years. Whatever the extent of the national contribution to policy formulation, opposition parties, intellectuals, trade unionists, and others assail policy reform (or structural adjustment) programs that they regard as imposed by donors—particularly of course by the Bretton Woods institutions.

Genuine internal debate is rare under these circumstances, and dialogue between donors and the host country is distorted and imperfect.

During a recent visit to Uganda, the author met with the Economic Committee of the Parliament to discuss privatization and other policy issues. Committee members said that debate over privatization policies was minimal. When the parliamentarians questioned members of the administration, they were told that there was not much point in such discussions, because executive branch members had no influence over privatization policies. These were negotiated with donors (negotiations in which they were not involved) and incorporated in policy loan agreement with donors.

Moreover, these parliamentarians could find out little about issues and problems. When officials or outside observers came before the committee, they invariably spoke as defenders of the existing program and policies. So the parliamentarians had practically no access to critical analysis. Although this may have been particularly true of privatization, it probably also happens in other sensitive components of reform programs. And Uganda in these respects must be typical of a great many low-income countries.

Efforts have been made to limit the negative effects of conditionality—by reducing the number of conditions, insisting on prior actions, and sharpening the conditions themselves to make them clearer, less intrusive, and more monitorable. But this does not seem to have changed things much. The number and complexity of conditions remains large, backsliding from prior actions compels additional measures, and intrusiveness does not seem to be noticeably less.

More unsettling, there are signs that donors who have been hesitant participants in the conditionality game, such as the EU and the Nordics, are beginning to use it more liberally. According to one recent analysis, the main impetus seems to be the view in the European aid community that many African Caribbean Pacific (ACP) partners lack the political will or ability to implement agreed-upon programs.[6] Aside from administrative weakness, this concern rests on the view that in numerous partner governments political and economic power is too concentrated; governments are not sufficiently accountable to their people. At the same time, division of responsibility for the use of aid resources between the EU and its ACP partners is poorly defined. As a result, the EU is introducing more conditionality, tighter and more formal rules, and more centralized management of its aid programs. In these circumstances, honesty increasingly demands insertion of the qualifier "so-called" whenever the term "partnership" is used.

■ ***Giving priority to donor agendas, which include increased aid effectiveness, is frequently incompatible with enhanced local ownership and local capacity.***

As is well-known, aid donors have their own development agendas, and these have tended to drive the agendas of the aided countries. Thus all the great swings in development orientation during the past 40 years were generated in the industrial countries and were transmitted through aid channels into developing country policy and program orientations. There were always divergences between donor and local priorities, but these usually could be reconciled on the ground. When donors invented integrated rural development approaches in the 1970s, for example, it was easy enough to refit existing agricultural programs into the new mold.

Reconciliation is harder today. Donors have introduced ambitious new elements into their agendas. They now seek better governance in its political and legal dimensions as well as in public administration. They stress direct attacks on poverty and give priority to gender-related inequities. They insist on slimming down the civil service and shedding state enterprises. They undertake public expenditure reviews and ask for removal of low priority budget items. They urge the opening of markets to more competition, subsidy removal along a broad front, and many other economic and institutional reforms.

Recipient countries, meanwhile, and particularly the most heavily aided of them, are confronted by crises of numerous kinds. Many are struggling for survival. Few have been able to achieve macroeconomic balance and stability. Most have been unable to prevent severe deterioration of basic administrative services. Only a few among the low-income countries have been able to generate much GDP growth.

Given the different perspectives of the partners in the aid relationship, it is hardly surprising that local ownership of much of the donor agenda is, at the most, lukewarm. Local decisionmakers and elites may not be opposed to donor-generated ideas on appropriate development strategies, but their ordering of priorities is likely to be different. Ownership is also lukewarm because local political leaders are much more risk-averse than aid agency technicians, and much of the donor agenda represents a challenge to established political and bureaucratic interests.

Alongside the divergence in priorities is a clash between donor concern to improve aid utilization and the goal of enhancing local capacity. The two conflicting goals are often linked. Thus according to one report,

> the European Union is now pushing to redefine the Lomé partnership so that its priorities will be better reflected in spending. . . . [Another] of their aims is to accelerate implementation, perhaps by reallocating some responsibilities between the partners—in this case, from ACP countries to the European Union.[7]

Pressures to attain planned spending levels and growing pressures to increase aid effectiveness (which emanate from both sides of the table) underlie many of the capacity-destroying donor policies. The heavy use of expatriate technical assistance for implementation of "their" projects impels donors to rely on expatriate technical assistance, most of it involving long-term resident experts. Experience has taught that this type of assistance rarely enhances local capabilities; it tends to upset internal staff relationships and is a poor vehicle for training.

As noted earlier, aid programs that are large relative to the size of the aided economy require lots of managing. Recipient public sectors are too thinly staffed and poorly organized to manage projects and handle the complex, diverse financial accounting and reporting requirements of the donors. In most cases, local officials find it easier to leave management to the donors. As a result, technical assistance is written into projects without much review. Much expatriate technical assistance is also brought in to service donor financial management and reporting requirements. These "gatekeepers" or "controllers" operate outside the governmental structure in most cases. They grease the donor aid programs. Their presence entails little strengthening of local capacity. At the same time, donors devise systems of direct and indirect payment to allow recruitment of skilled locals to work as project staff, with well-known negative effects on internal incentive structures.

Although there has been much talk in recent years about breaking out of this system, only a few serious attempts seem to have made up to now, and there are already signs of backtracking. During the 1980s the

Swedish International Development Cooperation Agency (SIDA) introduced recipient-led approaches to the management of this aid. In its "changing roles" policy, emphasis was on institution building and capacity development to ensure local ownership of projects and programs. This had a profound effect on SIDA's working methods. Within two years, procurement of goods and services by SIDA was cut in half and transferred to its partners along with training packages and manuals; long-term technical cooperation dropped by 75 percent; and management authority was delegated to the field. However, as SIDA tried to deal with demands for more aid efficiency and recipient transparency, this type of partnership began to be questioned. SIDA now seems to be leaning toward more control-oriented approaches that reduce the recipient role in the partnership.

■ ***A heavy aid presence is anti-capacity development because it allows local political leaders to postpone hard decisions, induces policy passivity, and distorts the policy environment.***

Perhaps the most insidious impacts of an extensive aid presence are on attitudes and incentives. Aid tends to "deresponsibilize" political leadership and induce a sense of resignation and passivity among national technocrats. The extent of these intangible effects is hard to know; their presence is revealed only by a few anecdotes and limited personal observation. But they are probably pervasive.

Various aspects of the deresponsibilization phenomenon can be pointed to. How can it be that so many poor country governments allow public administrations to suffer intolerable scarcities of the most basic inputs, such as paper, pencils, vehicles, and petrol? One reason is that donors can provide enough copying machines and paper and cars to allow administration to limp along. How can so many governments continue to avoid serious attack on the profound disarray that has marked their civil services for years? Part of the answer, again, is the aid presence, which indirectly finances staff though technical assistance, and which provides salary supplements and contracts for many of the best people.

A heavy aid presence redefines economic rationality and distorts incentives. Donors and local technocrats counsel governments to choose for inclusion in public investment programs only projects with a satisfactory economic rate of return. But why do that, when the supply of and demand for projects is such (or at least has been such) that funding can usually be found for any reasonably well-packaged proposal. Worry about debt service? Maybe, but the prospects for debt relief have always been good. Senegal and neighboring states were warned about future debt burdens when they pushed for donor financing of big dams two decades ago. They ignored those warnings. And they were right to do so, because most of that debt has already been forgiven. Worry about the recurrent costs enough to reject projects for which grant financing is in hand? Ridiculous. The reasonable posture is to accept all offers and hope that there will be more resources in the future or that donors will sustain the project once completed.

The insistence of some African governments that high severance payments be made to retrenched public employees, and their refusal to act unless donors finance these payments, illustrate another aspect of the responsibility/incentives problem. Programs aimed at needed retrenchment of public sector payrolls are often subverted on these grounds. Many liquidations or sales of state-owned enterprises have been held up for similar reasons. It is as though decisive action requiring political risk and a cost to some groups are only possible if donors pick up the financial costs.

The spread of attitudes of resignation and policy passivity is harder to document. Many technocrats talk about it. They say that the donor dominance in project programming and even more markedly in policy formulation and implementation gives them little or no real role. Why try to initiate policy interventions anyway, since World Bank staff or others will probably find it inadequate, and their own ministers are in any event mainly interested in satisfying donor requirements and not in encouraging indigenous policy initiatives. Passivity thus prevails among local technocrats, who in the majority of heavily aided countries do little more than take potshots at the policy proposals designed by donor technocrats.

IMPLICATIONS FOR AID STRATEGIES

■ IN LOW-INCOME COUNTRIES, aid inflows that are large relative to the size of the recipient economies have powerful antidevelopment effects.[8] "Large" can not be precisely defined but experience suggests that aid to GDP ratios of even 5 percent set in motion the institutional dynamics that undermine local capacity. It suggests also that institutional deterioration accelerates rapidly as aid ratios increase.

Donors should not let the risk of providing fuel to enemies of foreign assistance prevent them from recognizing that this phenomenon exists and incorporating it into their strategies. They should begin preparing their most aid-reliant clients and home constituencies for a different future, one in which official assistance has a much smaller role. They should set official targets—for example, that by the year 2010, no country should be receiving ODA that amounts to more than 5 percent of GDP. This may happen anyway. But putting this kind of target on the table would have many advantages. It would, for example, provide needed focus for donor-recipient negotiations such as those on the future of EU-ACP country relations.

An explicit and time-bound target of reduced aid dependency would create a different context for thinking about aid policies and a different set of pressures and constraints. It would stimulate fresh thinking and give a new urgency to the task of enhancing local capabilities. Shortcuts to institutional self-reliance would be sought and might be found. Fundamental problems that have seemed intractable, such as civil service reform and sluggish supply responses, would attract the attention and resources they demand.

All of this might happen in the normal course of events during the next decade. But it would be a mistake—for donors and recipients alike—to follow the habits of the past 30 years, and proceed as though the future volume of ODA going to the heavily aided countries will not be much reduced, or will even grow. Failure to confront explicitly and immediately the challenge of how to achieve a world of greatly diminished aid dependence discourages new thinking about the transition.

Some changes for effective transition come to mind right away. Capacity enhancement has to be given in reality the high priority that is lavished on it in rhetoric. This means that other priorities have to be downgraded. Thus in the frequent instances where the demands for faster and more effective program implementation lead to donor policies that undermine local capacity (heavy resort to expatriate technical assistance, widespread payment of salary supplements to recruit locals for staffing projects, stronger and more centralized controls, for example), the goals of maintaining given levels of spending and implementing individual projects more efficiently should be given much less weight than in the past.

Also, explicit conditionality should be abandoned or at least drastically reduced. This is partly to allow the development of local commitment and ownership of donor-financed programs and policy reforms. It is also essential for the emergence of greater political responsibility, including a stronger sense of the necessity of choice and the flowering of local initiative in policymaking.

The idea of dropping conditionality is hard for many donors to swallow. It would go down easier if the aid mix contained much less program (budget and balance-of-payment) assistance and more project-related aid. Program assistance is more fungible than project aid, at least in the conditions of the heavily aided countries, and hence requires closer control to assure "appropriate" utilization. The risk that economic assistance without conditionality would encourage governments to defer needed policy changes can be reduced by cutting the share of program assistance. Also, donors can maintain the implicit conditionality that now prevails: Countries that are good performers on governance and macroeconomic policy receive more aid.

The question of accommodating differences in donor and recipient country program priorities is perhaps more vexing even than the conditionality issue, and solutions are less evident. On some key substantive issues, accommodation seems relatively easy. The donor focus on poverty alleviation, for example, allows plenty of room for local leadership preoccupations of political survival and economic growth.

Issues of process or approach can be less malleable. For example, donor priority to assist nongovernmental organizations (NGOs) presents local governments with real concerns. On the capacity-building side, it is much like previous "bypass" modes—ways to go around inefficient or corrupt government agencies. This encouragement of private sector capacity is fine in principle: It complicates, however, the local governments' policymaking and regulatory roles. If 50 NGOs are doing microenterprise lending in Tanzania, without coordination on repayment policies, interest rates, or cost sharing, for example, policy direction is made much more difficult. It is the same with fertilizer distribution and food aid. Where numerous NGOs (or indeed official bilaterals) follow different price and subsidy policies, this not only complicates general policymaking but can threaten fundamental institutional objectives such as the nurturing of private sectors.

The general guideline during the transition should be to change the mix of aid instruments by giving greater weight to those that are institutionally unintrusive. Debt relief, for example, gets high marks on the intrusiveness criterion and should be applied to all the heavily aided countries. As noted above, policy-based lending and program assistance in general should be drastically reduced or abondoned in favor of expanded project aid. Although recognizing the desirability of assistance to civil society and the high priority for private sector development, implications for government regulatory and policy roles should be given greater attention.

This shift in aid approaches and instruments would take time of course. It would be much facilitated by the introduction of urgent programs to build project-making capacity. Generalized use of sector programming would help, provided that it is accompanied by broader harmonization and simplification of donor reporting and monitoring requirements. A too-rapid slowing of disbursements could be partially offset by increased spending on regional centers of excellence and by more intensive use of developed country institutions (in education and training, research, for example). Most important of all is the need for a broader and deeper dialogue between donors and low-income recipients, a dialogue about targets for self-reliance and how best to get there.

Notes

[1] This paper was presented at the Workshop on External Resources for Development of the Netherlands Economic Institute, Rotterdam, The Netherlands, May 1996. I am indebted to the Netherlands Economic Institute for permission to reprint this text, a version of which will be published in Olga Memedovic, Arie Kuyvenhoven, and Nico van der Windt (eds.), *External Resources for Development* (Norwell, MA: Kluwer Academic Publisher, forthcoming 1998).

[2] Not all process-related dimensions of foreign assistance are considered. The politics of aid are not addressed, for example, nor, except tangentially, most conventional political economy issues. Impacts of aid on macroeconomic performance—savings, consumption, investment, exports, growth, poverty, and income distribution—are also passed over.

[3] The aid data in this paragraph come from World Bank, *African Development Indicators 1996* (Washington, DC: World Bank, 1996), p. 315.

[4] Organization for Economic Cooperation and Development, Development Assistance Committee, *Principles for New Orientations for Technical Cooperation* (Paris: OECD, 1991), para. 27–28.

[5] See *The Courier of the European Community,* No. 141 (September–October 1993), pp. 48–84; and Peter Harrald et al., "Integrated Sector Investment Programming," World Bank Discussion Paper (Washington, DC: World Bank, 1995).

[6] Jean Bossuyt and Geert Laporte, "Partnership in the 1990s: How to Make It Work Better," Policy Management Brief No. 3 (Maastricht, the Netherlands: European Centre for Development Policy Management, December 1994).

[7] Bossuyt and Laporte, "Partnership in the 1990s."

[8] Possible negative impacts on domestic savings and on exchange rates are passed over here.

About the Authors

ELLIOT BERG is an independent consultant and Adjunct Professor at the Université d'Auvergne, France. He taught at Harvard University and the University of Michigan and was for many years Director of the Center for Research on Economic Development at the University of Michigan. He ran his own consulting firm in the 1980s and was Vice President for Policy Research at Development Alternatives, Inc., until 1995. He has spent many years in developing countries as consultant/advisor, researcher, and visiting professor, and has written extensively on varied development issues. He was main author of *Accelerated Development in Sub-Saharan Africa* (World Bank, 1981); and *Rethinking Technical Assistance* (U.N. Development Programme, 1993).

MICHAEL BRUNO, former Chief Economist of the World Bank, died on December 26, 1996. Prior to joining the World Bank, he was Professor of Economics at Hebrew University and the Governor of the Bank of Israel. He had also served as President of the Econometric Society and President of the International Economics Association. As a macroeconomist, Dr. Bruno was highly regarded by both his fellow economists and policymakers. He left an outstanding record of achievement and is missed by many admirers, including his coauthors for the paper published posthumously in this volume.

PAUL COLLIER is Professor of Economics and Director of the Centre for the Study of African Economies at Oxford University; Professor Associate of CERDI at the Université d'Auvergne, France; Associate of the Tinbergen Institute, Amsterdam; and Fellow of the CEPR, London. Dr. Collier works on a wide range of macroeconomic, microeconomic, and political economy topics concerned with Africa. He also serves as consultant to the International Monetary Fund, the World Bank, the European Commission, the Swedish International Development Cooperation Agency (SIDA), the International Labor Organization, and **DFID,** where he is on its **ESCOR** committee.

CATHERINE GWIN is Senior Vice President at ODC and directs ODC's international policy research program. Prior to joining ODC, she was Senior Program Adviser at The Rockefeller Foundation, on the staff of the United States' International Development Cooperation Agency, and Executive Director of the Council on Foreign Relations' 1980s Project. She is Vice Chair of the African Economic Research Consortium and a director of numerous nonprofit boards. She has written extensively on U.S. development cooperation policies and on the International Monetary Fund, World Bank, and other international economic and development institutions. With Mayra Buvinić and Lisa Bates, Dr. Gwin coauthored *Investing in Women: Progress and Prospects for the World Bank* (ODC, 1996), and with Albert Fishlow, Stephan Haggard, Dani Rodrik, and Robert Wade, *Miracle or Design? Lessons from the East Asian Experience* (ODC, 1994). Among her other publications are *U.S. Relations with the World Bank,* 1945–92 (Brookings, 1994); and *Pulling Together: The International Monetary Fund in a Multipolar World* (ODC with Transaction, 1989).

JOAN M. NELSON, an ODC Senior Associate, is currently completing a project as co-chair of the National Research Council Task Force on Transition Economies. From 1991 to 1994 she directed an international collaborative program on interactions between market-oriented economic reforms and consolidation of democratic openings in Latin America and Eastern Europe. Other recent projects include a major collaborative study of the politics of economic adjustment programs in developing nations; assessments of the use of conditional aid to promote political, environmental, and other non-economic reforms; the evolving roles of unions in developing and post-Communist countries and factors shaping union behavior in the course of labor market adjustment; the relevance to post-Communist nations of Third World experience with the politics of adjustment. Among her many publications are three recent ODC volumes: *Intricate Links: Democratization and Market Reforms in Latin America* (ODC with Transaction, 1994); *Global Goals, Contentious Means: Issues of Multiple Aid Conditionality* (ODC, 1993); and *Encouraging Democracy: What Role for Conditioned Aid?* (ODC, 1992).

MARTIN RAVALLION is Lead Economist in the World Bank's Development Research Group. He has written and advised extensively on poverty in developing countries and policies for fighting it. His recent publications include *Poverty Comparisons* (Harwood Academic Press, 1994); "Poverty and Policy" (with Michael Lipton) in the *Handbook of Development Economics,* Vol. 3 (North-Holland, 1995); and "Famines and Economics" in the *Journal of Economic Literature* (1997).

LYN SQUIRE is currently Director of Development Policy in the office of the Senior Vice President and Chief Economist of the World Bank. His career at the Bank has included terms in both Operations (Senior Economist for Indonesia; Lead Economist for West Africa; Chief, Country Operations Division, Mexico; and Chief Economist, Middle East and North Africa); and Research (Director, Policy Research Department; Economist, Employment and Rural Development Division; and Chief, Resource Mobilization Division). In addition, Dr. Squire was the Staff Director of the *1990 World Development Report.*

About the ODC

ODC is an international policy research institute based in Washington, D.C. that seeks to inform and improve the multilateral approaches and institutions—both global and regional—that play increasingly important roles in the promotion of development and the management of related global problems.

ODC's program of multilateral analysis and dialogue is designed to explore ideas and approaches for enhancing global cooperation, to build networks of new leadership among public and private actors around the world, and to inform decision making on selected development topics of broad international concern.

ODC is a private, nonprofit organization funded by foundations, corporations, governments, and private individuals.

Peter D. Sutherland is the Chairman of the Overseas Development Council, and the Council's President is John W. Sewell.

ODC
1875 Connecticut Avenue, NW
Suite 1012
Washington, DC 20009
(202) 234-8701
http://www.odc.org

ODC Board of Directors

CHAIRMAN

Peter D. Sutherland
Goldman Sachs International

VICE CHAIRMAN AND CHAIRMAN EMERITUS

Stephen J. Friedman
Debevoise & Plimpton

CHAIRMEN EMERITI

Theodore M. Hesburgh
University of Notre Dame

Robert S. McNamara
United States

Victor H. Palmieri
The Palmieri Company

DIRECTORS

Pedro Aspe
Vector Casa de Bolsa, S.A. de C.V.

Kwesi Botchwey
Harvard Institute for International Development

Margaret Catley-Carlson
The Population Council

Peggy Dulany
The Synergos Institute

Edward K. Hamilton
Hamilton, Rabinovitz and Alschuler, Inc.

J. Bryan Hehir
Harvard Center for International Affairs

Ruth J. Hinerfeld
United States

Anthony Lake
School of Foreign Service
Georgetown University

Pascal Lamy
Crédit Lyonnais

Timothy P. Lankester
School of Oriental and African Studies
The University of London

Edward J. Lill
United States

Donald F. McHenry
School of Foreign Service
Georgetown University

Harris Mule
Tims Limited, Nairobi

John W. Sewell*
Overseas Development Council

Humphrey Taylor
Louis Harris & Associates, Inc.

Willi A. Wapenhans
Germany

Clifton R. Wharton Jr.
Teachers Insurance Annuity Association/
College Retirement Equities Fund

Robert B. Zoellick
Federal National Mortgage Association

ON LEAVE FOR GOVERNMENT SERVICE

Stuart E. Eizenstat
Department of State

Nancy H. Rubin
U.S. Ambassador to the Human Rights Commission

COUNSEL

John B. Reynolds III
Wiley, Rein & Fielding

* Ex-Officio

Note: Affiliations provided for identification only.